Gladys Nicol

ATHENS

B. T. Batsford Ltd, *London*

For Doreen

First published 1978
© Copyright Gladys Nicol 1978

Filmset by Progress Filmsetting, London
Printed in Great Britain by
J. W. Arrowsmith Ltd, Bristol
for the publishers, B. T. Batsford Ltd
4 Fitzhardinge Street, London W1H 0AH
ISBN 0 7134 0627 5

Contents

Illustrations

All illustrations are between pages 77 and 92

Preface and Acknowledgments

Millions of words have been written about Athens over the centuries, many of them in most learned treatises, others which give descriptions of how the city looked at the time of a particular visit, and yet more which have used the city as a background for a romantic novel or an exciting who-dun-it. All of them have presented different views of the same whole, yet all of them are unanimous in finding this city an interesting and fascinating place, whose ancient stones must draw constant pilgrimage. So much indeed has been said, that it is difficult to find new things to say. The answer is perhaps, not to try, but instead, to present a more personalised view of past and present in order to intrigue the intending visitor or the arm-chair traveller sufficiently to spur them into delving into the many great works which line the library shelves and which can bring so much informative pleasure in their own right. If I can perform even that small service to a city which has given me so many happy times, I shall be content.

But no book can be written without much assistance from other people, and first and foremost I would like to thank the National Tourist Organisation of Greece, particularly Peter Analytis, Yanna Kioufi, Cleo Angelopoulos and Sia Moraitou for their tremendous help and encouragement, and Kelvin Moyses who has been a tower of strength. There are many people working in the tourist industry who have delved into files and produced facts, figures and practical assistance, and among these must be mentioned, Bazil Mantzos and Ron Ellison, Adele Biss, Doug Goodman and Chris Economides, of Olympic Holidays, Thomson Holidays and Olympic

Airways respectively, and members of the staff of Cosmos and Cosmopolitan, who went to considerable trouble on my behalf, Stuart Rossiter for his immense knowledge of Greece, so freely shared, Nina Nelson as a constant provider of newspaper cuttings, Margaret Tyrrell for patient proof-reading, René Longeval for his generous and sympathetic skills, and many more whose names are not here but to whom I owe a great debt of gratitude for their sustained interest over a long period. And finally, may I thank my many friends in Greece whose kindness spurred me on to write about their capital city with deep and abiding affection born from their consideration for me.

Gladys Nicol

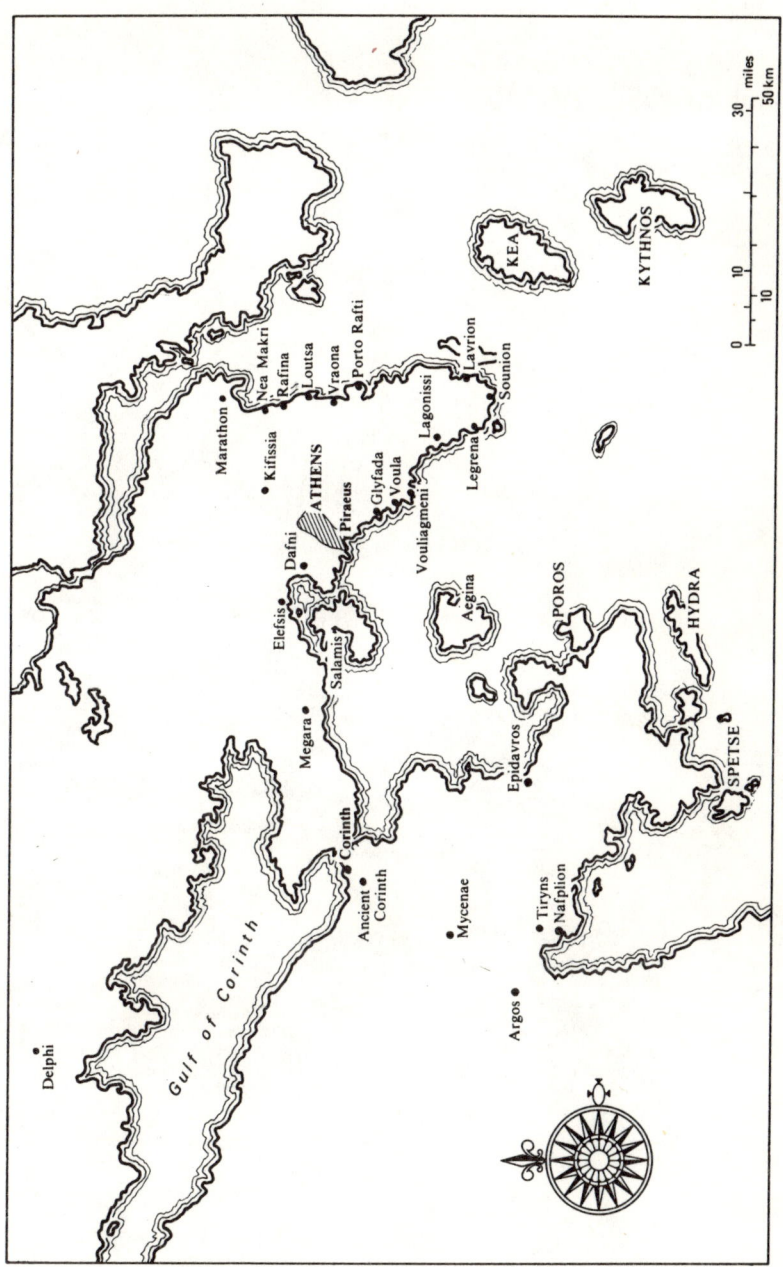

30 miles
50 km

KEA

KYTHNOS

10

10

0

Nea Makri
Rafina
Loutsa
Vraona
Porto Rafti

Lavrion
Sounion

Marathon

Kifissia

ATHENS

Lagonissi

Glyfada
Voula

Vouliagmeni

Legrena

Piraeus

Dafni

Elefsis

Aegina

POROS

HYDRA

Salamis

Megara

Epidavros

SPETSE

Ancient
Corinth

Corinth

Gulf of Corinth

Mycenae

Tiryns
Nafplion

Delphi

Argos

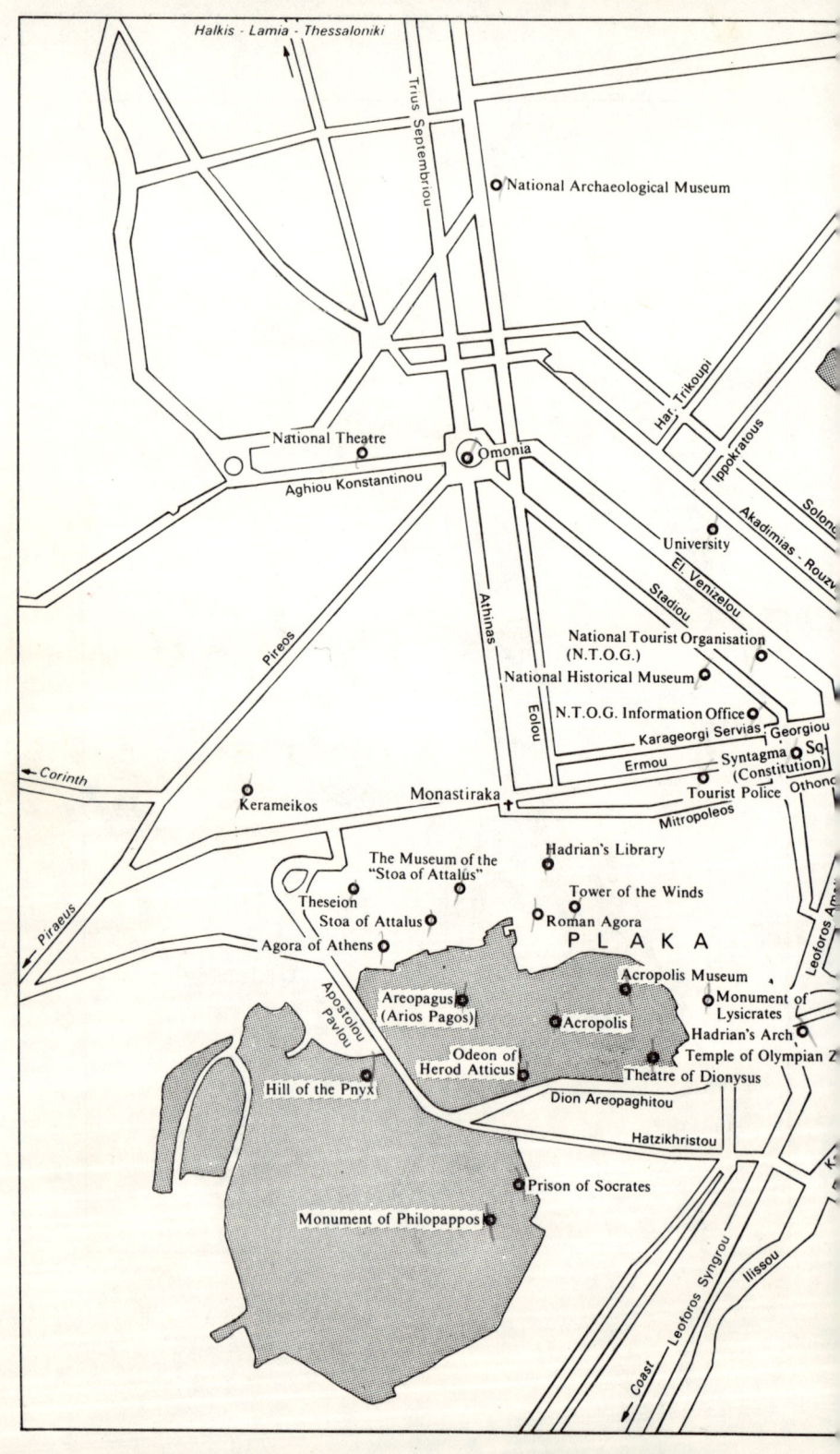

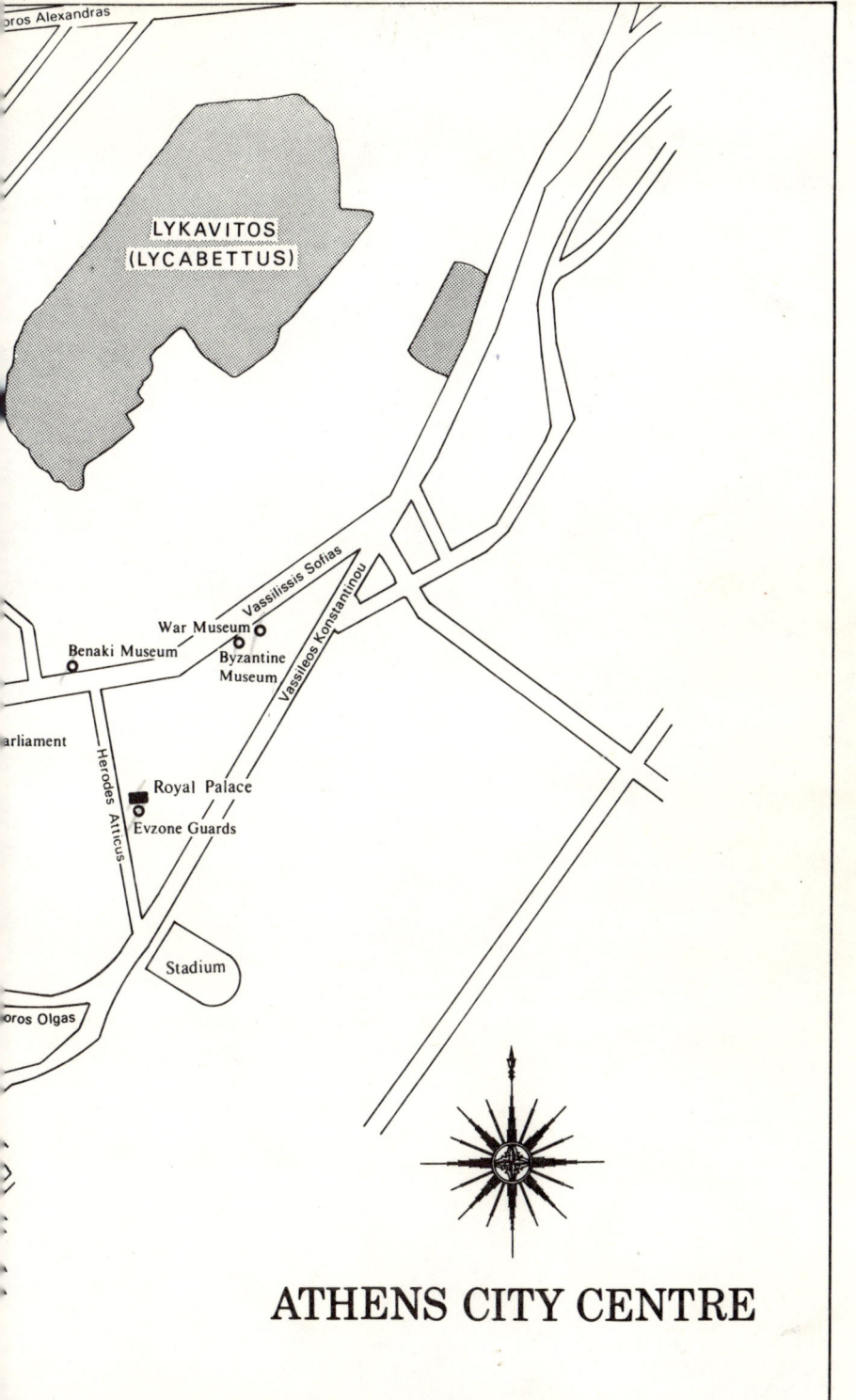

ATHENS CITY CENTRE

1 Synopsis of a city: History

One Sunday afternoon early in November, two of us sat at a a minute table on the crowded terrace of the cafe which nestles close to the summit of Lycabettus Hill in Athens. There were a few other foreigners around, but mostly our neighbours were Greeks, enjoying the gentle autumn sunshine sipping endless cups of their beloved thick black coffee and the inevitable accompanying glasses of water. There was a constant stirring and clinking, conversation hummed, and people promenaded on the balconies and up and down the shallow marble steps which lead to the little chapel of St George crowning the hilltop beside the great bell. Groups posed in frozen animation before the persuasive click of family cameras before melting again into the laughter and intimacy of the entirely Greek scene. It reminded me that despite the millions of visitors who throng her streets, tramping the tourist circuits with the relentless enthusiasm of reforming angels, Athens still belongs to the Athenians, and that, away from the fleets of buses, taxis and touts at the foot of the Acropolis, and the often spurious atmosphere of the Plaka, it remains largely unknown to the modern invading armies. Perhaps this is due in no small measure to the fact that the city has been accustomed for nearly 4,000 years to a constant coming and going of people over her doorstep. Few came in friendship, so the inhabitants developed a shell within which they could live their own lives with as little disturbance as possible, while at the same time preserving a friendly and welcoming exterior to all comers. The habit persisted even when the city reached international status, and although Athens is not Greece (for no capital can claim to be entirely representative of its country) it is very Hellenic, and its hospitality is as fine as anywhere else in this lovely land of blue water, white houses and courteous people. But Athens still hides feelings deep within itself. It is not given to many outsiders to glimpse that inner life, still less to partake fully of it. Even small slices of everyday happenings are precious peeps behind the scenes, and this Sunday interlude was for me a case in point.

Somewhere around 400 years after the birth of Christ, Synesius of Cyrene wrote that 'The Athens of today possesses nothing ... except the famous names ... which remind one of old Athens as the hide of a slaughtered beast reminds one of the former living creature.' Nearly 1600 years later, the 'Athens of today' looks to the casual observer or to the first time visitor, to be in precisely the same condition. The straggling mass of greyish houses, shops and factories crowd in upon one all the way from the chaotic airport terminal at Hellenikon despite the brilliant presence of the sea, while, from the docks at Piraeus, impressions are even worse. There, two cities run indivisibly into each other in a muddle of domestic and commercial living on either side of a road ribbon where traffic is indescribably noisy, drivers inexcusably impatient, and one looks in vain for the glowing city of Pericles and the seats of learning that St Paul knew. But, in this moment of disappointing discovery, we are only echoing the sentiments of many who have trodden this same path over the centuries before our pre-packed tourist-orientated era.

Horace called Athens vacuous. Ovid said 'only the name is left'. In the nineteenth century, an English traveller called the city 'barbarous'. All are right, yet all are terribly wrong. Walk, early on a Sunday morning, between the more elegant apartment blocks in the Kolonaki, and 'empty' is the right adjective. The squalid districts which grew from the Asia Minor exodus in the early 1920s bear no resemblance to the Athens of Timon. The Easter barbarity of selling day old chicks within red plastic 'egg' prisons still continues despite some public outcry. Yet, as you hurtle by taxi on the merry-go-round of Syntagma Square, jostle in the Near East atmosphere of Ifestou and Monastiraki, along with all the other tourists, or watch family parties gossiping around the tiny pond in the Zappeion Gardens, you are conscious that this is a living city, deserving more than a cursory glance at its untidy modernity before hurried departure for the serenity of the islands. And when, through the summer dust haze and the exhaust fumes, or as the wind whines from a winter sky, the gleaming skeleton of former glory is revealed, you know that the Athens you dreamed of is there, waiting within your own imagination and, from the words left to us through the ages, you may clothe those bones in magnificent living flesh. From that moment, there is no turning back. Athens, as the Ancients, the Franks, and the Turks, knew it, lives within the Modern City, and, as you get to know them all even in a modest way, a love/hate relationship develops which in turn enchants and aggravates for the rest of your life.

After the Greek War of Independence, the decision in 1834 to appoint Athens as the capital city of the newly fledged nation was a wise one and not entirely due to the glories of the past. After all, there were, and are, many other equally beautiful and famous remnants of the old civilisations stretched over the breast of Greece like proudly worn medals on an old campaigner.

The main reason lay in the practicality of its position. Facing the Saronic Gulf, within easy reach of some of the best harbouring on the Eastern Mediterranean on the existing trade routes of the time, between East and West, it was also ideally placed to give accessibility from every point of the land and sea mass of the kingdom. With the advent of the aeroplane, the wisdom of the choice became even more apparent, not only for internal communications but as a link in air travel chains across the world; one can reach Athens from anywhere in Europe in but a few hours.

Its climate is on the whole a kind one, and although, in common with the rest of the world, general patterns seem to be changing slightly, there are longer sunny days and less fluctuations in temperature than in more northern climes. Summers are hot, and can be sticky, and visitors soon join the general exodus to the beach areas, though it is seldom that locals immerse themselves in seawater before the beginning of July. It is left to the mad foreigners to bathe from May onwards! By October, when tourists are still in short sleeved light clothes, most Athenians are wrapped in heavy woollies and winter coats from which no amount of persuasion can coax them, and by January one understands their reason. Days are often gloriously sunny, with brilliant blue skies and long periods of sunshine, but winds are bitter and the peasant habit of drawing a scarf across nose and mouth is a wise one to emulate, for the cold bites down into the throat like a knife. I once was unwise enough to climb to the top of Lycabettus Hill on a January day, and got a dose of bronchitis for my pains. . . ! But now that we are back at this dominant feature, let us stay for a moment and look at Athens from a distance.

She sprawls untidily around the base of the hill engulfing lesser slopes of the many smaller protuberances, so that their summits stand out on the off-white city carpet like inkstains on an Indian rug. She lurches towards the waters of the Saronic Gulf, and in the other direction loses herself hopelessly in the haze which envelops Mount Parnis. Perhaps legend was right, for it says that the Goddess Athena dropped this hill to the north-east of the Acropolis in order that her city might have protection. It certainly affords a grand vantage point from which to spot possible marauders; I strongly advise it as the point from which to commence any assault on the more interesting historical strongholds for the city lies like a map at one's feet. Mind, distance is deceptive. It looks but a short walk between any of the classical remains. It has been my experience that, on a long hot dusty day in high summer, every step of the way seems like 100 miles, and without a doubt, if you intend to sightsee, the best time of all is in springtime, when the winds have gone, the air is cleansed and sweetened before the summer dust arises again, and the sun gently warms bones chilled by northern snows, allowing sightseeing and walking in comfort, though a jacket is necessary most evenings. Excursions too are pleasanter in spring, for despite the extension of the tourist season into year round activities, the Attican countryside wears its best dress of mimosa blossom and spring oranges while country tavernas have their usual fringe of regular customers at the outside tables instead of hiding them away in dark interiors. And perhaps, best of all, the custodians of antiquities and the shopkeepers whose livelihoods depend on the favours of the tourists have had a winter rest from silly questions and awkward requirements, and look more favourably upon the new crop of seekers after truth and bargains. This is not to say that one does not receive great courtesy in most encounters at any time, but it has been borne in upon me over a period of years that by November and December the people who work in the service industries are beginning to show the strain of the very long seasons. The tourist industry has become one of the mainstays of Greek economy in recent years, and has been responsible to a very great extent for the improvement in the standard of living for a large number of people, but it has not been accomplished entirely without cost. Much of that cost has been in the loss of the sense that foreign visitors are still something of a novelty. . . .

That really cannot apply to Athens if one is honest. Foreigners have been making their way to the Acropolis—the city on a hill—and to the surrounding, less attractive city below the walls, since time immemorial, and what's more, have been writing about their findings for almost as long. So many books have been written about Athens during the centuries that it is virtually impossible to find 'new' things to say, but it is possible to make the reading a little lighter, and to dress the findings in fresh attire rather than the uniform of classical knowledge, which can be a little difficult to digest if only making one brief sortie to the city. For longer and more prolonged stays and for probing thoroughly into the past, it is essential to refer to the many splendid and learned works available in great variety. But today's visitors come for the most part by air, and aeroplanes

~~have a habit~~ of depositing their human cargoes at their destinations at ungodly hours with the result that tourists often get a most distorted first view of the places they've travelled so far to see. Tired, fretting at further delays while they and their baggage are piled into bus or taxi, the new arrivals view the unfamiliar horizons with jaundiced eyes, hating the deserted streets and only longing to crawl into the protective cocoon of their prospective hotels. But, sometimes, there are compensations in these somewhat dampening arrivals, and Athens, despite its chaos, its general air of seediness and the complete incomprehensibility of its road and neon signs, never fails to provide its quota. It may be that a tall column appears and disappears like a wraith in the bus headlights, or that arrival coincides with a full moon, so that the Acropolis floats like a mirage above the sleeping city or, in early morning light, blushes pink while the watering carts sweep pathways to her feet. Whatever it is it lifts one's vision above yesterday's refuse still littering the pavements, and the human debris lurching their way uncertainly homeward, and all ugliness is forgotten in the promise of immortality. It is at that moment, whether one visits for the first or the umpteenth time, that there comes the realisation that Athens owes so much to the gods and goddesses of antiquity who inspired the creation of tangible dwelling places among their devotees, and that, to begin to understand the complicated city that is to be found in the Athens of the classics, even in the miniscule amounts possible for the layman, it is advisable to know something of the family tree of the Immortals. Even then, as in all families, there are so many skeletons rattling in cupboards and endless versions of the behaviour of 'baddies' and shining examples alike, that one can be completely mystified. There is a distinct danger of getting sidetracked into some particular story that attracts, or of getting bogged down in detail, or worst of all, finding so many variations that it becomes easier to give up all effort and simply admire the statuary and temple trimmings for themselves.

But that would be a pity. Except for the serious

archaeologist or architectural buff, half the fun attached to antiquity is to relate these stories to the figures and to try and understand why such and such a god was chosen, say, to stand for eternity over a certain shrine or tomb. I suppose it can be likened to the passion for reading graveyard epitaphs in modern times, but it has the distinct advantage of not condemning one as morbid. The precedent has been set by too many famous names to allow that, so let us, too, start as far back as we can.

Creation has puzzled Man since he was able to think for himself, and almost from the time he reared himself on his hind legs, he has had to believe that some other being ruled his destiny rather than blaming all his mistakes on his own fallibility. After turning from the original and primitive worship patterns, it was perhaps natural that the Greeks set up the image of a divine family who controlled Man's actions. Disasters such as earthquakes or floods were far more easily acceptable if attributed to the laughter or sorrow of the gods rather than to the complicated workings of great natural forces, about which they were, largely, ignorant, and in any case Man has always believed that in the beginning there was—Chaos.

From Chaos emerged Mother Earth, or Gaea, and she somehow produced a son, whose name was Uranus, or Heaven. He looked upon his naked mother and was so ashamed that he wept and, as he wept, rivers, seas and lakes came to cover part of her nakedness. These in their turn produced flowers, trees and even animals, and in time, Greece became the centre of Earth. As only Heaven and Earth existed, the niceties of being mother and son were ignored and their union produced a family of monsters. Firstly came hundred-handed triplet giants, and secondly another set of triplets, the one-eyed Cyclopses. The whole family were flung into the furthermost corner, called Tartarus or the Underworld, and Heaven and Earth tried again.

This time, they got the Titans, who looked more or less normal. But handsome is as handsome does and, urged on by their Mother Earth, (who no doubt was tired of the efforts and results of Heaven's advances), they fell upon Heaven while he slept and castrated him with a sickle shaped knife. They divided the world between them under the leadership of the youngest Titan, called Cronos (Time). Mother Earth begged him to set the Cyclopes free, but having taken one look at them and at the elder brothers, he sent the whole brood back to the underworld.

Naturally, Earth was furious at this treatment of her elder sons and in revenge, she prophesied that Cronos would in turn be dethroned by one of his sons for, by this time, Cronos had married his sister Rhea. Cronos swallowed each child that Rhea bore him, and his wife, understandably, became annoyed with this habit and appealed to her mother (cum mother-in-law) for advice. When the sixth child arrived, Rhea wrapped a large stone in swaddling clothes and like a dutiful wife presented the bundle to her formidable husband. Being shortsighted he devoured it without noticing the difference. The surviving infant was named Zeus (Jupiter), put into the care of the she-goat Amalthea, and hidden in the cave of Dicte, high in the mountains in Crete. He was brought up there, along with his foster-brother Goat-Pan. In gratitude to his foster-mother, Zeus eventually set her image among the stars, and we can see her there as Capricorn.

In due course, and with the connivance of Rhea, Zeus was appointed to be cup-bearer to Cronos, and availed himself of the opportunity to administer an emetic which caused even that iron-stomached monarch to vomit. First came the stone, quickly followed by the children. The stone became the centre of worship at Delphi, and two of the elder children, Poseidon and Hades, helped Zeus to depose their father. The three then drew lots for the division of his possessions. Zeus won the skies, Poseidon the seas, and Hades the underworld. But the earth was left as common land, though officially Zeus had the final say on contentious happenings. The main reason for the latter decision was that, even in those days, might was often held to be right, and Zeus had a goodly supply of the atom bombs of the time, in the form of thunderbolts forged by the newly released Cyclopes. It was this deadly stockpile which eventually forced the Titans to acknowledge Zeus's supremacy. Cronos, of course, hadn't taken all this change without protest, and for ten years there was terrible war in Thessaly, when mountains were piled one upon another in an attempt to reach the abode of the new gods, but, finally, Cronos met defeat and, they say, was sent to Britain....

Atlas, leader of the rebellious Titans and second in command to Cronos, was given the job of holding up the skies for evermore, and the remainder of the Titans were sent back to Tartarus. Mother Earth had in the meantime been quite busy, and brought forth yet another of her hideous creations. This time it was Typhon, and although Zeus hurled his thunderbolts at him, it wasn't until Mount Etna came crashing down on Typhon's head that he was hidden from view. He's still there, spouting smoke and flame in defiance and generally behaving as a thoroughly bad character to his human neighbours.

One of the Titans had remained on Zeus's side through all this time, and his name was Prometheus (Forethought). As a reward he was given the task of creating Man, and he did this in the image of the gods themselves, using clay and water as his materials. Man of course had to work, but with the work came Sin, and as punishment Zeus took away Fire, which had been lit by the Sun's rays. Prometheus couldn't bear to see Man suffer, and brought more Fire, but Zeus would brook no disobedience, and chained poor Prometheus to a mountain where an eagle tore his liver for eternity.

Zeus, by means of a trick, had married his sister Hera, and they set up house on Mount Olympus, after spending a lengthy wedding night, lasting 300 years, on the island of Samos, and thereby producing two sons and one daughter, Ares (Mars) god of war, Haphaestus (Vulcan) god of blacksmiths and Hebe, goddess of youth, but the parents quarrelled incessantly, mostly over Zeus's predilection, not only for other goddesses, but for the human women which had

~~been fashioned after the flood which had engulfed the earth~~
as another punishment. The heavenly marriage guidance
councillor, in the person of Aphrodite (Venus) Goddess of
Love, who had sprung naked from the sea, even lent Hera
her magic girdle, but apart from managing to produce
several more children, either to each other or by other
partners, they continued to bicker as before. They still do.
Haven't you heard them throwing the crockery? Well, you
probably thought it was a thunderstorm. . . .

But it could not all have been Hera's fault, because
apparently Zeus became so unbearable that even other
Olympians revolted and tied him in rawhide with 100
knots. But, typically, they then all quarrelled over who
should be boss, so Thetis, the sea nymph, set one of the
giants to untie the knots, a very easy task for he of the
hundred-hands.... It was Thetis, by the way, who eventually
married a mortal king, Peleus, father to Achilles.

Another marriage was between Poseidon (Neptune) and
Amphitrite, but apart from Triton, the merman, their
children were an undistinguished breed and little is said
about them. Perhaps it is as well, for they might have inherited Poseidon's rapacity and illtemper, both causes of so
many quarrels with other immortals, when he elected to take
over their domaines. Most of the time he did not succeed,
but even today, you'll see him nibbling incessantly at other
people's territory.

Goddess Demeter was sister to Zeus and Poseidon, but
that didn't give her immunity from the advances of her
amorous brothers. Poseidon raped her once, but it was to
Zeus that she bore a daughter Persephone, and it was this
pretty girl who caught the eye of Hades, who abducted her
while she was picking flowers. The distracted mother
searched the earth's surface for her, but it was not until she
reached Eleusis that she picked up her trail. The king's son
had seen a chariot, drawn by black horses, racing down a
bottomless pit and the driver had been holding a struggling
figure in his arms. Demeter realised what Hades had done,
and instantly forbade anything to grow on earth in retribu-

tion. It was only after compromise that the earth was allowed to bloom again, and this meant that Persephone spent three months of each year with Hades, and the rest with her mother. Thus we have the change of seasons. As a reward for his information, which in modern parlance 'led to the apprehension of the criminal', the king's son at Eleusis was shown the art of agriculture, and how to plant corn. Hence the temple to Demeter at Eleusis, of which some small remnant remains.

One of Zeus's amorous pursuits involved Leto, but in usual fashion, after getting her with child, he lost interest, despite the fact that the affair had incurred Hera's displeasure. She forbade Earth to grant Leto asylum, and sent a serpent, Python, to harry the poor girl, now nearing her labour. Poseidon pitied Leto and gave her a floating island called Delos, and it was here, leaning over a palmtree so it is said, that Leto gave birth to Apollo and Artemis (Phoebus and Diana). As reward for his efforts, Python had been given the guardianship of the sacred cave at Delphi, and when Apollo grew to manhood, he avenged his luckless mother's tribulations by slaying the Python and setting up the Pythian Games.

The legends about Artemis are rather mixed. She had become a huntress and amused herself by shooting silver arrows at huntsmen and animals alike, but she had also been confused with the older Moon Goddess. Appollo, too, has taken over from the Sun God Helios, whose statue bestrode the harbour at Rhodes, and was known in antiquity as the Colossus. Their morals seem to have been as dubious as their parents'. Artemis loved Endymion, a shepherd and Orion, a hunter. The first was put permanently to sleep by Zeus whilst the second she shot by mistake, due to some intrigue of Apollo, who thought Orion was getting too enamoured of Eos (Dawn), his handsome boy attendant. Orion too has been placed among the stars.

Aphrodite (Venus) came into the Goddess business via the Orient and wasn't of Zeus's family tree. Her followers used the Syrian traditions of temple harlots, though this was not continued much in Greece apart from the Corinth temple. She was also jolly mean with the loan of her girdle and as punishment was married to Haephestus, the least attractive of Zeus and Hera's offspring. Indeed, he was so ugly that as a baby Hera had dropped him off Mount Olympus and it had been left to Thetis to rear him, but he was of a forgiving nature. He released Hera from her chains when Zeus had punished her for her part in the rebellion but when father discovered what he had done, he threw him from Heaven where he landed on the island of Lemnos and was lamed.

It was Haephestus who discovered Aphrodite and Ares *in flagrante delicto,* and threw a net over them and left them on public show. Hermes and Poseidon liked the view, and when released, Aphrodite spent the night with Hermes as reward, bearing him Hermaphrodite. The name speaks for itself. Then, after doing the rounds with Poseidon and Dionysus, she went back to the sea at Cyprus, and became a virgin again, truly a remarkable achievement under the circumstances. During all this activity, she had also managed to have another son, though, not unnaturally, no one could be sure who the father might be. His name was Eros, and eventually he fell in love with Pysche (Soul). Their daughter was, most appropriately, called Delight!

There were the illegitimates too. Hermes, for instance, who became the messenger god, and the protector of travellers, was the son of Zeus and Maia, the daughter of Atlas. Dionysus was another son of Zeus, this time by Semele, daughter of the king of Thebes. He was born in miscarriage when his mother died of shock ·after seeing Zeus in all his glory as a god, and was sewn into Zeus's leg and delivered on time three months later. This is why he was given the name 'twiceborn'. He eventually married Ariadne on Crete.

Apollo seduced the princess Coronis in Thessaly but, killing her before her time for infidelity, seized the baby and gave it to a Centaur for safekeeping. The child eventually became the God of Healing, Asklepios, whose main temple was at Epidaurus. And then there were the nine Muses, daughters of Zeus and the Goddess of Memory,

Mnemosyne, who dwelt on Mount Helicon, but came, according to Homer, to inspire him on the slopes of sacred Olympus.

There were many more...Minos of Crete, Sarpedon, Epaphus, all descended from Zeus, but, most important for our story, there was Athena, though her antecedents were hardly promising. True to his normal atrocious behaviour, Zeus seduced his aunt, the Titaness Metis, but then, finding she was pregnant, he followed family traditions and swallowed her. Either due to repentance, or an appalling headache, he asked Hephaestus to hit him on the head with an axe, and, when his skull was clove in two, Athena sprang, fully armed, and fully grown, from her father's head. Although she was an excellent soldier, she disliked war for its own sake and would only support just causes. This wisdom, which she had inherited from Metis, was to stand her in good stead, as we shall see. I have told you of Poseidon's bad temper and greed. He also had his share of the family traditions of incest, rape and seduction and when one thinks about it he seems to have few good qualities. Certainly none which would be worthy of loving worship, but he is always symbolised as the most manly of all the gods. Perhaps the ancients were playing safe in worshipping out of fear or a desire to hedge their bets. Or perhaps, in the perverse manner which attracts even the most levelheaded of women towards a bad hat while being fully aware of his faults, they were drawn by his deceptively attractive exterior. After all, what could be more beguiling than the Aegean Sea in its sunniest mood, yet it contains myriad tiny jellyfish who wait to torment human invaders, as I have discovered on more than one occasion!

Poseidon's kingdoms stretched along the coast of Attica (or Achaea) and he espied the city on an inland hill, called Kekropia, which had been established by Kekrops, a mighty Phoenician. The god coveted the city, but Athena, adult from birth and therefore wiser for her years than one might think, also liked the look of the city. Uncle and niece quarrelled fiercely on the issue of 'top god', and took the matter before the Olympian Council. Each contender was asked to produce some proof that their claim was the greater, and, anxious to establish his authority and have done, Poseidon struck the earth with his trident. It is at this point that two divergent stories unfold. One says that Poseidon produced a fountain sea. The other that he produced a magnificent horse, symbolising all his own undoubtedly handsome virility. You must choose your own version when you visit the Erechtheion, but remember them.

Whichever way it was, it was then Athena's turn. Unshaken by all Poseidon's majesty, she produced an olive tree, because, she maintained, peace and prosperity and the cultivation of olives were better for man's development than the warlike pursuits of which she was undoubtedly capable, warrior goddess that she was. The logic of her action won the day, and from that time, Kekropia was renamed Athens in honour of its patron goddess. Poseidon of course retired to his main temple at Sounion where presumably he presided 'happy ever after'.

All this mythology may seem to be frivolous when applying it to some logical sequence of events in the history of a great city. But it is quite necessary, particularly when admiring some of the magnificent remnants of ancient Athens, whether Greek or Roman, to have some idea of how the Great Ones fitted into the scheme of things, for it all affected human imagination, particularly in the Golden Age in the depiction and glorification of the gods who presided over mere man's destinies. When it comes to historical fact, then we must again look into the clouded mirror of time.

Athens was certainly known to Neolithic man. The slopes of the Acropolis had natural water supplies and, standing 500 feet above the plain, could be defended from marauders. From the Mycenean age, that is from 1500 years before the birth of Christ, there was a fortress, and several well-preserved fragments of wall, known as Cyclopean, are still visible. Homer refers to the 'House of Erectheus' where the worship of Athena began. Theseus is given the credit of unifying the surrounding country of Attica into one state, making Athens the capital, but it was not until the 6th century B.C. that the area had an agricultural and economic footing, when Solon used the silver mines at Laurion to give the new city-state a sound currency, reorganised the Constitution and introduced a People's Council to work alongside the Areopogates Court, thus commencing the two house principle, which to date we have maintained.

The Persian invasions at the beginning of the 5th century, under Darius, were long, and difficult. The battle of Marathon in 490 B.C. started the turn of the tide in favour of Athens, but it was ten years later in 480 B.C., that Xerxes came to avenge his father's defeat at that battle. During that decade, the Athenians weren't idle. Themistocles insisted that the silver mine revenue should be put into the building and equipping of a fleet of triremes and also upon the strengthening of defences of Athens and the Piraeus. There were many voices raised in protest as there will always be when money is spent on armaments rather than on social welfare schemes, but Themistocles had his priorities right. The wisdom of his decision was realised when Xerxes advanced his forces upon Athens, for despite the stand of the Spartans at Thermopylae he eventually stood before Athens itself. Then, the Athenians fled to the ships, leaving their homes and possessions to be stripped at leisure, but they, as a people, remained intact. Within a few months, the opposing forces met at the great naval battle of Salamis with complete victory for the Athenian fleet. This was followed by a land battle at Platea, and then by the battle of Eurymedon, so that Persian hopes were extinguished.

Even while Athens lay in smoking ruins, Aristides set up the alliance between her and the Ionian Greeks which resulted in the formation of the Delian League. This was a brilliant stroke, for as Athens grew in power, she forced the islands to pay tribute in return for protection, eventually insisting that the League Treasury should be transferred from Delos to the Acropolis in 454 B.C. One interesting facet of this is that in that same year, when the Panathenean procession took place in honour of Pallas Athene (Athena Polias) it was decided that the 'allies' would have the right to send suitable trophies and representations to join the procession every four years, a clever way of binding highly superstitious peoples into a fear of offending the all-powerful goddess if the pattern was changed. In the meantime, the foresight of Themistocles had been put to further use. He supervised the building of the Long Walls, running from the Pnyx and Mouseion hills to Piraeus, which offered better harbouring and strategic value than the port at Phaleron, and even more important for us, he arranged the rebuilding of Athens city walls. To do this, he used much of the rubble remaining from the former buildings, and so preserved for posterity many fragments of the city which had stood until the Persian destruction.

It is often said that necessity and inspiration are frequent bedfellows, but it is also certain that a great deal of advantage is obtained when the right men are in the right place at the right time. The strongest leader of one of the many powerful families was Pericles, and he, fortunately, was a man of vision and ambition. He was also beset with the immediate problem of finding work for the population who had flocked back after the wars, and for the returning soldiery. The one complemented the other. Money from the Delos Treasury was safely and immediately available. The city was ripe for development. Many great sculptors and builders were awaiting opportunities, so Pericles entrusted the work to his great friend Phidias, a master craftsman who was made responsible for co-ordinating and planning. This brilliant man had the wisdom to use Pentelicon marble for the great buildings of the Prophylae, Parthenon and the Erechtheion, an act which must call down the blessings of every artist or photographer who has tried to record the Ancient City, for the marble changes colour according to the time of day and mood of the skies. I have seen it almost luminous in moonlight, blindingly white at midday, grey, golden, or cream in winter, autumn and summer, and even flamingo pink at sunset.

It is amazing, when we look at the chronology of the Golden or Classical Age, that it was so brief, for quite apart from the structural achievements, it has handed so much down to us. It opened up many new avenues of thought and expression. It gave us in the western world the basis on which our civilisation stands, and it was responsible to a very great extent for the power of the dramatic arts, so therefore, in direct line, it has pointed the way for all our present media. Before the Golden Age, there was no drama as we known it. It had originated long before in peasant rituals, songs and dances used in the service of the god of the vine, Dionysus. In these celebrations, a goat was sacrificed to the god and voices recited the stories of the god's sufferings on behalf of man. The ritual was called Trag-odia (Goat's Song), and partly due to Thespis, the whole art form had changed into Attic Tragedy. It was this stylised presentation which changed yet again in the Golden Age, under the influence of dramatists such as Aeschylus.

The Golden Age started its descent into oblivion with the death of Pericles in 429 B.C. though it see-sawed for years afterwards. There was the rule of the Thirty Tyrants, the loss and then the restoration of the Constitution (obviously not a habit confined to modern Greece) and the continued glorification of Athens. Plato, Demosthenes, Socrates and the master sculptor Praxelites, all move across the turbulent canvas of the era.

However, in the north, a new menace had arisen. Philip of Macedon marched southward, and conquered the Athenians at Chaironeia, but fortunately his son, Alexander the Great, was lenient with the city. The beautiful buildings, garish with the colourings of the day, were added to and extended, while Aristotle, Alexander's personal tutor, held sway in the Lyceum. When Perseus was defeated in 168 B.C. by the fast-rising Roman Empire, Macedonian rule ended and the Romans took over the city. For a while, the city retained all its status and privileges, but when the Athenians attempted intrigues with other enemies of Rome, General Sulla razed the walls and looted much of the treasures.

By the time that the Apostle Paul came to Athens in 54 A.D., it had become the university city of the Roman Empire, content to leave military ambitions and political intrigues to others, intent only on its elegant and respected course as the seat of learning, and upon the daily gossip which formed its main entertainment. It was not even the capital of its province (named Achaia under Roman rule) for Corinth had that privilege.

But although the powers of Athens had disappeared, her buildings had not. Rather the reverse, for the city was still the centre of the old religion with temples and shrines to every one of the Ancient Gods. St Paul tells us that there was even an altar to the 'unknown god', and he took this for his opening gambit when he first preached to the Athenians. The practice of dedicating an altar to an unknown god had been in use for several centuries, and there is an interesting little anecdote about it. It seems that there had been a terrible plague in Athens, and that, despite sacrifices on every altar, it continued unabated. There was a prophet in far-off Crete, called Epimenides, and he was asked to help in the city's plight. He drove a flock of sheep to the Areopagus, and let the animals stray in every direction. When they chose to rest at length in various places, the sheep were sacrificed 'according to the fitting god'. The plague ceased, and the whole of the civilised world of that time commenced the custom of setting up altars to these unknown beings.

One of the first indications of the final demise of pagan Athens was given by St Paul. He said that the old ways were condemned because of the narrowness of the base on which they were constructed. At first none listened. None, that is, except, we are told, two people. One was a woman called Damaris, though of her we know nothing. The other was a member of the all powerful Areopagus council, whose name was Dionysus and who became the first Bishop of Athens, and who is believed to have suffered martyrdom during the reign of the Emperor Domitian. There is another story about

Dionysus which I like. It says that Dionysus went with St Paul to Rome, and after the Apostle's death, went to France, where he met his own execution on Mont Martre (Hill of the martyr) and became, eventually, St Denys, Patron Saint of France.

Most of the Roman emporers liked Athens and contributed towards the further glorification of a city which was already becoming morally and spiritually degenerate. Hadrian has left the most lasting evidences of this Roman contribution. He lived there as often as imperial duties would allow, and as we shall see when sightseeing, erected the Great Arch on Amalias Avenue (Leoforos Amalias in Greek), was responsible for the building of the Library, and as the completion of the great Temple of Olympian Zeus was completed during his reign, it was he who performed the dedication ceremonies.

After all the efforts of the 700 years it had taken to build it, the temple was not allowed to stand in one piece for very long. Credit for its destruction is given by some authorities to the Gothic invasions, although opinions vary, according to which sources are tapped. It is inevitable that discrepancies must creep in. In view of the alarums and excursions which have taken place over the centuries, it is constantly remarkable to me that any information is constant at all, yet in his fascinating book, *Old and New Athens,* Demetrios Sicilianos records that there was an Athenian historian, Dexippus, who lived at the time of the Heruli/Gothic invasion and who had recorded all the historical events from the time of Alexander until Emperor Claudius Gothicus, but that none of his work has come down to us. Sicilianos also tells a delightful little anecdote of the Goths who, about to set the library aflame, were ordered by their leader to spare it because the Athenians were such easy prey due to their pre-occupation with books.

During that period, Christianity was making some inroads into Athenian life, and in one way this was not to be wondered at. The city had become much poorer, and the new religion brought more consolation to the poor than the pagan ceremonies could with their undoubted appeal to richer elements. The date of the Christianisation of the Parthenon is only approximate, but it is sure that the Olympic Games were suppressed in 393 A.D. on the grounds that the athletes' nudity offended strict Christians, and it must have been at about this time that the heathen temples were finally closed by Emperor Theodosios. By the time that the Emperor Justinian prohibited the teaching of heathen philosophy and law, and closed the schools in 529 A.D., Athens was indeed a shadow of its former ebullient self and many of the great statues had long disappeared.

Byzantine rule would, but for two incidents, have meant the almost total absence of mention of Athens for hundreds of years, though, after the sack by the Slavs around 580, there cannot have been much left. Emperor Constans II wintered in the city in 662, harbouring his fleet at Piraeus before leaving for his attack on the Lombards in Sicily in the following spring, while the infamous Boris II celebrated his terrible and bloody victories over the Bulgarians with a thanksgiving held in the 'Church of the Mother of God' (the former Parthenon) in 1018 and I cannot think that She would have been particularly pleased by this blithe supposition of Her partisanship.

The Emperor, who was instrumental in restoring much of the Byzantine glories, blinded 15,000 prisoners of war before sending them home to Bulgaria as an example to his newly conquered province. We are told also that he made suitable presentations to the Church of Our Lady of Athens, in the form of lamps and a golden dove. We are not told if he got them from his war spoils. . . .

In spite of being such a poverty stricken, almost forgotten place, Athens seems to have had an archbishop, for, when the Byzantine Empire, in its turn, fell to the Franks and Boniface the Third of Montferrat received the title of King of Salonica (Thessaloniki), there had been an archbishop, Michael Acominatos, who lived in his official house on the Acropolis. He had been instrumental in keeping the fierce Lord of Corinth from appropriating Athens when that gentleman had sought to profit by internal troubles in the Byzantine Empire. Acominatos went into retirement when Boniface arrived and eventually died in the Monastery of St John the Baptist on Kea.

For a century, the House of de la Roche ruled over Athens, but made little or no contribution to it. Indeed, they chose a small monastery some miles from the city walls for their family burial place. This was the former Byzantine monastery at Daphni (Dafni) which had been Byzantine until the Cistercian monks from the Burgundian order were given the building by the de la Roches. But if they added nothing, they at least brought peace and chivalry to the area, and took nothing away, and for that we owe them thanks. During their century of rule, Thebes was, for a time, capital of the related houses of La Roche and St Omer, for it was a city of great propserity, mainly due to a flourishing silk industry. It also seems that there was religious and racial freedom under Frankish rule, for Jews and Genoese were permitted to settle in Thebes and the monks of the Greek Church were also permitted to follow their own worship.

With the death, in 1308, of Guy II, the rule of de La Roche ended, and the title passed to a Walther de Brienne, killed three years later in the battle of Kopais, when the Grand Company of the Catalans destroyed the power of Frankish Greece in a day, and assumed command. The unfortunate Walther had originally hired the mercenaries of the Catalans to help him in waging war against the triple alliance of Constantinople, Neopatra and Arta, but it was rather a case of riding a tiger, for, once successful, Walther had wished to pay them off, but they firmly declined to leave. The inevitable battle took place between Walther's cavalry and the Catalans on 15 March 1311, the Catalans being outnumbered by five to one. But the ground chosen at Kopais was marshland and the horses sank under the weight of men and armour so that most were killed by a rain of arrows. The Catalans laid waste to Thebes and then took over Athens, as well as the unlucky wives of the fallen knights. We know little of the sojourn of the Catalan Company but we do know that they turned for protection to Frederick, king of Sicily, and that during their rule marriage between Greeks and Catalan conquistadores was forbidden. We know also that the Catalans destroyed Corinth and, perhaps most interesting of all, that the son of Walther, Cautier de Briene (who was to die at the battle of Poitiers in 1356), still called himself Duke of Athens and tried, unsuccessfully, to get his lands back in 1351.

With the arrival of the Florentine Nerio Acciajuoli (Acciaioli) at Megara and Piraeus in 1386, new owners moved into the duchy. He was later given the title of Duke of Athens, and there is a letter in a library in Florence which states that 'on May 1388, sire Nerio took the castle Setines' which was the name by which Athens was known. He set up his capital in the city, and during his rule, and that of his natural son Antonio, many Albanian shepherds came as settlers to the Attican province, replacing the many Greeks who had been carried off by intermittent Turkish pirate raids, so that we see that even then there was good cause to fear the depredations of the Turks on those coasts. It also accounts for the incursion of the Albanian tongue into the dialects of the islands.

Florentine rule lasted only 60 years, much of it under the protection of Venice who had interpreted the rather peculiar terms of Nerio's will as an excuse to seize Athens. For us, it is interesting to note that the ducal palace of the Acciajuoli family was the Propylaea and that a second floor was added at that time. They also erected a tall watchtower made of remnants from other buildings on the Acropolis, which stood until 1874 when the Acropolis was cleared of much of the accruing debris of the centuries in a resurgence of national pride.

Nerio II married twice. First to the widow of his cousin Antonio, son of Nerio I. Second to Chiara whose son Francesco was of course then the rightful heir, but whose position was usurped by a cousin, Franco, at the order of Sultan Mehmet II, the powerful overlord. Poor Chiara met a sticky end at the hands of Franco, for, when she was kneeling in prayer in the church of Daphnú, he beheaded her with a sword. This is not irrelevant in the history of Athens, for, when the Sultan heard of the incident, he ordered General Omar to march upon the city and take it from Franco. The Acropolis surrendered in 1456 and thus began the Turkish domination of Athens which lasted, apart from brief periods, for the next 400 years.

Turkish rule produced dreadful privations, but when one looks at them with hindsight and against the background of the customs of the times and the general Near Eastern attitudes towards anyone they considered inferior, frightful though they were, they were little different to hardships and horrors endured and written about elsewhere. Throughout the four centuries (and though the violence varied from era to era and the population suffered greatly) there was never any real attempt to completely suppress the Greek Orthodox religion, probably because this would have contravened Koranic law, which forbids interference in other religions. Instead, the regime used the heads of the Church to issue edicts through and put the onus on them to extract obedience. In consequence many of the traditions and customs of the Church were able be preserved and a strength of purpose endured.

Other conquerors will come and go, but the bitter subservience of those centuries furrowed deep into the Greek character and will take equally long to erase. But let us go back to the beginning of that time for a moment, for in history, as in any romance, it is fascinating to know 'what happened next'. The story continues with Franco, the last of the Acciajuolia, who was executed in 1460 by order of the Sultan, his wife sent to the Sultan's harem, and his three sons, Matteo, Jacopo and Gabriele made into janissaries, but, two years before that terrible fate befell them all, Sultan Kehmet arrived in Athens on his first visit, receiving the keys of the city from the Abbot of Kaisariani. In return, he ordered that the monastery, which still exists and may be visited, should only pay symbolic tax.

It must have been a few years after this visit by the Sultan that the Church of Our Lady of Athens, which has been built inside the Parthenon, was transformed into a mosque, because, in 1466, when the Venetian Admiral Vittorio Capello managed to take the city for a brief period, though the Acropolis remained in Turkish hands, someone whom I can only presume to have been a war correspondent of the day wrote that the Tower of the Winds which was later turned into a monastery or 'tekke' for the Dervishes, was still a Greek church, and that, although he couldn't get into the Acropolis, he could see that the Parthenon was still a Christian church. He also referred to seeing the 'old Palace' (the Propylaea), which was later turned into a residence for the military governor, with the Erechtheion housing his harem. I've always felt *that* was a strange turn of events for a temple dedicated to 'virgin' goddesses! Incidentally, Demetrios Sicilianos, whose knowledge and research must have been immense, says that the same correspondent reported seeing the stone lion at Piraeus which gave the port its Venetian name of Porto Leone. Perhaps it was that mention of its existence in 1446 which inspired Francesco Morosini to remove it to the Venice arsenal after his battles in 1689/90.

As long as the world has been turning, people have made their way across the face of it by various means, and on their return, often many years later, regaled willing listeners with their tales. Turkish-dominated Greece had its fill of overseas visitors many of whom had read of the glories of classical Greece and were anxious to visit these places for themselves. Of course they required souvenirs much as present day tourists do, and were willing to pay well for them, even though many of them were fake. But for the famous, the highly placed and the wealthy, there was always the real thing. For example, the English Ambassador in Constantinople collected on behalf of Charles I. The story runs that the fine collection of statues, some 400 in all, was too difficult to transport to England, so all the heads were cut off and taken instead. Sicilianos claims that this 'explains the presence of so many fine heads in the West and so many headless statues in Greece'—an interesting theory.

In 1537, when the French fleet anchored in Piraeus, as allies of the Sultan against the Venetians, at least two serving members must have written home about it, for their accounts have survived. One got as far as the stone lion at Porto Leone but couldn't be bothered to go to Athens. The other, an officer, La Borderie, wrote that 'Athens, once worthily called the flower of the world, has now . . . sunk to being the poorest and most miserable of cities. The wonderful buildings and great theatres are ruined and are turned into small dwellings. . . . I saw one theatre that time has not managed to level, supported on marble columns. . . . The Athenians have turned it into a church, erecting a curved wall inside that seems of later date.' He may have been referring to the Thesion.

The centuries that followed were terrible ones in Athens' history, for while escaping some of the awful tribulations which befell Greeks in other areas, disease and ignorance reaped their harvest and, in addition, they had to pay the child tribute required every few years. This involved the roundup of children of both ages between 10 and 12, the girls for harems, the boys for either eunuch or janissary service. One sentence, written in 1606, says it all. 'In 1543 in April, they took the children from Athens. Likewise in 1547, 1566, 1559 and 1666.' The picture is horribly familiar to those who remember the Nazi extermination processes. No wonder there were revolution attempts, though none were successful and always carried frightful reprisals.

But, even in this sad picture, there was one romantic little corner, for it was given to a young Athenian girl—Vasiliki—to be the means of sparing her city from the worst terrors. She was chosen to enter the seraglio of the Sultan, and was given the name Johahi. Sultan Ahmet soon began to call exclusively for her to come to him, and instead of using her position to make money from the eternal string of petitioners who sought the Sultan's favour, as most of the other women did, she asked him to put Athens under the care of the Kislar Agha, or Chief Eunuch, Governor of the Sultan's harem. This meant that all monies deriving from the city could go to the coffers of the harem and that if any of the tax-collectors or 'voivodes' as they were called, practised any illegal extortion. Athenians would have the right of direct appeal to the Chief Eunuch. It didn't always work in favour of the citizens, even if they won their case. On one occasion, after a deputation had successfully interceded in a case of unjust tribute, the infuriated Turkish collectors vowed vengeance and eventually killed the leader of the returning representatives, Michael Limbonas.

However, if the Venetians are anything to go by, I cannot think that the Greeks would have fared much better under any other invader. It was at the beginning of 1684 that the Republic of Venice declared war on Turkey, and sent Morosini at the head of an expeditionary force, as well as a mercenary band under Konigsmark. The Venetians were welcomed by detachments of Athenians who wanted freedom from the Turks, but at the same time mistrusted the newcomers. The attackers set up their guns on the Pynx, the Areopagus and the Hill of the Muses, and if you stand on the ragged surface of any of these you will realise how well placed they were for cannon emplacements against the door of the Propylaea, even with the erratic firing mechanisms of the day. Unluckily, one shell hit a powder magazine and fired the Propylaea, and on 26 September another went through the roof of the Parthenon, which had been turned into an ammunition store, blowing the building to ruins. It is claimed that the shell had been fired without orders by an Italian. The garrison surrendered, but the Venetians broke faith with the terms agreed, and attacked and raped Turks and Greeks indiscriminately.

Plague had been rife in Athens, so in that same year, Morosini elected to depart from the city and abandon it to the returning ravages of the Turks. However, before leaving, he decided to remove some of the reliefs from the wrecked walls of the Parthenon, and take them to Venice. Thanks to the ineptitude of the removal, the marbles fell, shattering into irretrievable pieces, so instead he took three lions. One was from the Acropolis, one from the Theseum, and the third, the most famous, the one which had stood guard at the harbour of Piraeus. They still keep vigil in Venice, their origin almost forgotten. . . .

By 1760, Athens was removed from the care of the Chief Eunuch, and, after a brief period under the Bey of Livadia, was auctioned yearly to the highest bidder. This put the inhabitants at the mercy of anyone who could afford to pay the price, and from that time conditions worsened, particularly when the Russo-Turkish war broke out. But wars, and occupations, have their heroes. It would take a book, and has done, to record them all, so perhaps I may be forgiven for only drawing attention to one incident. A poor young Athenian gardener was accused of participating in the revolutionary rising under Motromaras. It was, of course, customary to buy pardons if one was rich, but the young man had no resources. He was sentenced to die, but offered his life if he would become Moslem. He answered that he would prefer to die Christian than live Turkish. He knelt, made the sign of the Cross, and cried 'Strike for the Faith'. He was Michael Baknanas, eventually to be canonised as St Michael, first of the new Martyrs of the Liberation. Incidentally, the end of the Motromaras rising was tragic. Nothing came of the Russian promises of help, the group scattered, and were finally betrayed. The men were killed by slow torture on sharp sticks, the women were sold into slavery. But the worst period of all Athenian history under Turkish rule came during the Governorship of Hadji Ali Haseke, who came to the city in 1775. For two long decades after that the city was subjected to extortion, torture and murder to a degree never known before. Then, after an unsuccessful attempt to murder the Abbot Dionysus, the Hadji was exposed for the sadist he was and was executed, by order of the Sultan, on the island of Cos. Benizelos comments that 'thereby our country was delivered from tyranny, against all hope and expectation'.

From that period, until the stirrings of the Revolution in Patras, we have little of moment to record, yet, with hindsight, it would emerge as a most vital period in the long story of Athens, and of Greece. It was during this period that Lord Elgin, British Ambassador in Constantinople between 1799 and 1803, obtained permission to remove some of the friezes and fragments from the ancient buildings left on the Acropolis — an action which brought many outcries against the Ambassador, not least Lord Byron's, but there are, however, several factors in Lord Elgin's favour. We must give him credit for acting out of the highest respect for Greek art. He saw that the buildings were going to disintegrate completely under Turkish rule, and at that time, he could not have foreseen the possibility that Greece would shake herself free from foreign rule. His motive, was certainly the preservation of at least some of the relics of ancient Greece, though it must also be admitted that he wanted to perpetrate a little oneupmanship against the French, who also had their eyes on the treasures.

In the event, he lost a considerable part of his personal fortune in the process. It cost him about £75,000 to collect treasures from various parts of Greece and send them to Britain, where a parsimonious government gave him the princely sum of £35,000 for them. Many of his contemporaries among travellers to Greece were critical of his actions and suspicious of his motives, though perhaps we might in turn suspect them of a certain jealousy. Certainly the French consul, M. Fauvel, was known to be in this latter category, because he considered that he had more knowledge of Greek archaeology than any of the others. After all, was he not stationed in Athens? The British had no such niceties, and the influx of tourists merely highlighted the fact that they had thought fit to appoint a vice-consul in the person of a Greek doctor, Makris.

There were no inns or hotels for travellers to stay in on arrival in the city, and until there were foreigners lodged with their own consuls, or in the Franciscan monastery which stood near the junction of Lysikratos Street. Among the Britons were Lady Hester Stanhope, The Marquess of Sligo, The Honourable Frederick North, later Earl of Guildford and a Governor of Ceylon, and an ardent Philhellene all his life, and, of course, Byron. When he arrived in 1809, the good Greek doctor Makris had just died, and his widow and daughters eked out a living by letting rooms, so Byron was directed to the house. It was one of these daughters, Teresa, who Byron immortalised in his poem 'The Maid of Athens', and it is probable that he first developed his love and his knowledge of the Greek tongue along with attraction to the young Teresa, during his ten week stay under their roof. The next year, Byron came to Athens again, but on that occasion he stayed in the monastery where he wrote much of 'Childe Harold'. There is no doubt that it was Byron who brought the plight of the Greeks to more public notice in England, though others later were equally active. The Princess Caroline, wife to the Prince Regent, later George IV, and long estranged from her hard drinking, wild living spouse, was an admirer of Byron's work, and visited Athens in 1816, giving much money to the poor of the city. A record of her sojourn can be found in a book which was published in Paris in 1821. Perhaps it is not entirely coincidental that its publication came in the same year as the start of the Revolution. Publishers as well as writers often have an excellent sense of timing!

It was on 25 March 1821 that Germanos, the Metropolitan of Patras, in the Peloponnese, raised the Greek standard at Lavra, but it was a month later before Athens itself was attacked. After severe fighting the Acropolis was taken, but was abandoned after attack by a Turkish relief force. Again fighting was heavy, again a Greek flag appeared on the Acropolis in June 1822, and so it continued, not only in Athens, but all over Greece, with fearful losses on both sides. In May 1827 the Acropolis was again taken by the Turks and it continued in their possession until well after Independence was declared.

The newly hatched Greek nation considered that they needed a king, and began to look around the numerous royal families of Europe. Leopold of Saxe-Coburg was first choice, but there were still arguments about Greece's boundaries, let alone internal disputes, so this came to nothing, and Leopold later became King of the Belgians. The Greeks finally plumped for Otto of Bavaria, son of King Ludwig, and the new kingdom was established. In 1833 the capital moved from Nauplion to Athens. No city could have begun such an important function in less promising circumstances. The War of Independence had destroyed even the shabby town that had crouched under Turkish rule; there were no roads, no schools, no hospitals, most of the inhabitants had fled, and those that remained huddled in mean huts among the rubble of the antiquities. It was immediately obvious that something had to be done to make it a fitting habitat for a new king and his court, and although many German planners came in the wake of Otto and his young Queen Amalia, it was the design presented by Cleanthes and Schaubert, two architects who had been approached originally by the provisional Government to whom we owe the shape of the centre of modern Athens. It was based roughly on a triangle between Ermou Street, Piraeus Street and Stadiou, but later was extended into a polygon and incorporated the Royal Palace and Syntagma Square. It was, naturally, designed to suit the horsedrawn traffic requirements of the day, and it is miraculous that it copes even as well as it does with Greek driving pressures today. However, its main asset for present generations is that it also includes provisions for parks and open spaces of which Queen Amalias Gardens and the Zappeion are examples. Originally laid out to remind the royal exile of her homeland, they still provide a welcome retreat for citizens and visitors alike from the freneticism and dust of the incessant traffic.

Otto did not last long. There was revolt against him in 1843, when his absolute monarchy was changed to constitutional rule, and in 1862 another revolt brought his deposition and he died in exile. The next candidate was Prince William of Denmark, who became George the First in 1863. Since his assassination in Thessaloniki it has been his descendants who have intermittently resided at the newer Royal Palace on Herodes Atticus Street. Right from the emergence of the new Greece, it is difficult to follow the muddled patterns of the political scene and as a casual observer I would not attempt to do so, except to comment upon happenings where they affect the necessary knowledge of the city by today's visitors. The neat little German patterned city left as the legacy of Otto's rule was touched little by these events, and as the architectural details rapidly became adopted as 'Typically Athenian', many of the buildings added later possessed decorative touches which match the lacy balconies and fretted stonework of the originals, and for the rest of the nineteenth century and the early years of the twentieth, regardless of internal political happenings, Athens was still a pleasant city where the famous Acropolis received constant attentions from internationally eminent archaeologists and where travellers had arrived in increasing numbers. I mentioned the numbers of travellers in Greece before the Revolution. Immediately after the declaration of Independence, conducted tours began, and the first guidebook, as far as I can ascertain, was brought out for this 'mass market' in 1840. This was called *A Handbook for Travellers in the Ionian Islands, Greece, Turkey, Asia Minor and Constantinople* and was published by John Murray — Byron's publisher. Also, Christopher Wordsworth, the first Englishman to have been presented to King Otto in 1833, published a work devoted to Athens and Attica, in 1837, which was 'very well received'. They have continued without halt ever since!

The First World War was to change the image of Athens for good. After a spell of occupation by the Allies, which was opposed by the pro-German Royalist troops, the Treaty of Lausanne embodied a clause agreeing to the exchange of Greek and Turkish nationals. There were far more Greeks in Asia Minor than Turks in Greek territories, and over a million homeless destitute people descended on their capital city, setting up shantytown slums on the city outskirts and in the vicinity of Piraeus where they came ashore in droves from the transports. Conditions were frightful. Housing, if it can be called that, was built from oildrums and tarred paper, there was little water, even less sanitation and sickness and dysentery were rife. Although in time the flimsy structures changed into more permanent buildings much remained equally ugly so that the overall effect remained the same. The tragedies during the Second World War, and the Civil War which immediately followed it, added to the burdens, and although Athens now has a great deal of industrial development and new housing springs up in rapidly extending suburbs along reasonable roads (one effect of tourist expansion) the impression of an untidy, somewhat seedy city remains. It is another strange quirk that I have noticed in many places, that any architecture which comes in the aftermath of wars is exceedingly ugly.

In the light of all the changes which have taken place on the soil which now holds modern Athens, it is hardly surprising that one can find little resemblance among today's citizens to those classic creatures in chiton and himation which are immortalised in the friezes and statuary, and which, by featuring largely in our school history lessons and books, may have called up our own desires to see the so-called cradles of Western civilisation. One could probably better find examples of original Athenian stock in some of the remoter islands where at least a few must have fled over the centuries. The Athenians we see in streets, cafes and buses are the descendants of emigrants from every corner of Greece, from Albanians, Venetians, Franks, and Turks (and inevitably some Britons) who have intermarried and stayed within Athens' boundaries. Even the oldest and most respected Athenian families with famous and distinguished records in the service of their city can be put into the category of, shall we say, Pilgrim Fathers. General habits, mannerisms and certainly food are culled from this heteregeneous mixture. But the amazing and important fact that the Greek Othodox religion has maintained its form and stayed remarkably free of outside influences throughout all the vagaries of overlordship must not be forgotten either. It gave a continuity and a strength to a nation which, without its religion to cling to, must have disintegrated long ago. Fortunate circumstance or Divine Intervention? Each must believe what he will, but for anyone who has the good luck to be in Athens at Eastertime, sensing the strength of the unity of the everyday people as they flock to churches and into the streets with the candlelight processions, knows that, come what will, Athens will survive. After all, by changing its outward form with each wind that blew, whether from East. West, North or South, it has already stood for over 3000 years. It is unlikely to change the habit now.

The more recent political unrest, military rule, dictatorships, monarchy and republicanism, have brought many difficulties for Greece and more particularly Athens, for a capital is always close to the happenings of the moment, whether good or ill. The effects and the outcomes are too close in time to stand inspection in any detail, but if they have given anything at all to the nation, it must be that they taught a discipline which was not previously obvious. It is noticeable now that people are far more willing to talk freely of their experiences and feelings and are almost universal in being glad to be able to do so without fear of arrest, imprisonment and punishment. Long may it last. But it is to be hoped that they do not just as quickly forget the lessons so painfully learned.

2 Ancient Athens

It was a cloudy windy afternoon in spring when I parked the car on a side road along the main street named after St Paul — Apostolou Pavlou — and walked across the grey stone hill-side behind the point of the Areopagus which looks towards the Acropolis. There were several people scrambling or standing on the ancient summit but I sat down on the further-most spur, waiting for a small streak of blue sky which promised to appear overhead, so that the sun would highlight the tall columns of the Propylaea which faced me. As usual, and even as it was in antiquity, the steps were a mass of people on their pilgrimage to the Ancient City on the Hill, which is the translation of 'Acropolis', and, as I marvelled once more at the pale classic beauty of the remaining columns, I was saddened by the toll our 'modern environ-ment' takes of the stones. Already the buildings have suffered more from the air pollution which has been in-creasingly present in the last 25 years and from the feet of modern tourist pilgrimages, than from the previous 2000 years of ravage by conquerors, weather conditions and time itself.

The air pollution has come from several sources. The highly concentrated motor traffic of Athens and the in-creased industrialisation of the capital have played the largest part, but also there has been a considerable amount of damage from the forms of domestic heating used in the small houses immediately below the rock. Most of these house-holders are poor, and have no money to install different methods of heating their homes, so, despite a law forbidding the use of Mazout, the petroleum residue which gives off noxious sulphur dioxide, the practice continues, and is highly likely to do so for some time to come. In any case, it is the traffic which is the greatest offender. Coaches and cars still climb to within a few hundred yards of the temples.

Part of the solution therefore lies in the removal of many precious transportable items to the safety of indoor premises, and at the time of writing, the Caryatids from the Erechtheion, and pieces of the Parthenon statuary are already out of further harm's way in the Acropolis Museum, until a new museum is built below the hill on a site currently occupied by a police barracks. Far more complicated are the other problems, involving the structures themselves and the rock upon which they stand. Repairs over the last two centuries to the joints between the marbles have caused further serious deterioration, the surface of the rock has been worn to a smooth patina by the constant tread of boots and shoes, and to make matters even worse, no one knows the real stability of the rock.

All these things will have to be dealt with, in some cases by virtually taking the stones apart and reassembling them, and it is going to take a long long time, incredible patience, and an immense sum of money. As a first step, access to the interior of the Parthenon and to wings of the Propylaea is forbidden, and it is likely that visitors will be kept to authorised pathways. But at least the immediate impression will be the same as it has been for many years, as casts and replicas are installed in place of the real thing.

In spite of this comforting reassurance, I am very glad that I was able to visit the Acropolis while the ruins were all reasonably *in situ*. Probably, Spon, Wheler, Stuart, Revett, or any of the other travellers who saw these famous walls in their true magnificence when the Parthenon's roof was still intact would have felt the same.

When St Paul stood here on the Areopagus, his eyes saw the Acropolis in all its painted, gilded finery, but I could not help wondering how his mind saw it, for despite its array of gods and goddesses, this city was godless. He left us a clue in his speech to the Court of Elders, which we are told, met here on the Areopagus. 'Ye men of Athens, in all things I perceive that ye are somewhat superstitious', and goes on, 'God dwelleth not in temples made with hands. . . .'

The Areopagus was so named for the God of War, Ares (Mars). The ancients claimed that it was on this place that he had stood trial for the murder of one of his sons, and further down the hillside is the Cave of the Furies, who had the task of punishing wrongdoers. Logical as always, the Greeks thought this was a fitting place on which to hold their court. After all, if the accused did not agree with the verdict, he could, if he was fast enough off the mark, run down and seek sanctuary with the Furies whose frightening appearance was calculated to put anyone but an innocent man off going to them! It is not possible to get into the Cave now, and it seems to have become a repository for all kinds of debris, but mostly, it appears to me, Coca Cola empties. . . .

From the top of the Areopagus there is a flight of steep steps leading to the car and coach park, and from there it is easy to start the long walk upwards to the Propylaea, past the touts, the periptero, the postcard sellers and the tiny post office, to the ticket office by the Beule Gate, named after the famous archaeologist. There are usually a horde of half-wild cats living precariously on this hillside, existing on the half-eaten sandwiches of the tourists (picnicking within the Acropolis is forbidden), and probably keeping the rat population down in return. The shining steps are rather slippery and I would recommend that anyone intent on visiting the Acropolis wears non-slip sensibly heeled shoes as well as leaving any extraneous items, such as souvenir parcels, cardigans etc, in car or bus. But do remember the extra film for the camera. Nothing is more frustrating than finding out at the crucial moment that the new roll is 300 feet back down a hillside and that you know that the coach driver has gone to lunch with the keys in his pocket!

This shallow shining staircase has history in every stone. This was the route taken centuries before the birth of Christ, by the pilgrims in the Panathenaic processions, when a long saffron coloured piece of material was taken to clothe the xoanon, the wooden statue of Athena Polias which was said to have descended from Heaven itself. In those days, the steps were a ramp going straight to the gateway at a gradient of one in four. By the time of Pericles, it was as wide as the five gates of the Propylaea, and you can still see the marks made by the wheels of the chariots. After the Beule Gate, you will see sections of medieval and Turkish walls, and can still see a section of a rampart which dates from Mycaenean times.

Propylaea means 'porticos', and was the name given to entrances used for ceremonial purposes. Designed by Mnesicles at the request of Pericles, it was never finished. At that time there were several sanctuaries close to this spot and their authorities objected on religious and no doubt, political grounds. You will see that the building consists of a central hall containing the portal, and two wings. Behind is the vestibule, which at one time had a heavily gilded and painted ceiling, but during the seventeenth century it was struck by lightning, and as I have already remarked it was damaged again during the Venetian bombardment. Schliemann, that indefatigable gentleman to whom we owe most of the Myenaen finds, did undertake some repairs on the Propylaea, and so did Pittakis, but it was not until the early part of the present century that there was any real attempt to restore the central hall, and the wings were not restored until after the Second World War. You can find one of the columns, and a portion of the ceiling in position and there are also traces of paint on one of the nearby panels. You have to remember that it was, in every way, a painted city. Buildings were heavily adorned with brilliant colours, particularly blues, ochres and gilt and were not the delicately tinted marbles we see today. The women too were painted and classical writings are full of references to eye paint, rouge and coats of white lead. The habit persisted over the centuries, for even in 1675, Sir George Whele wrote that the women were 'so horribly painted that it was hard to conjecture their natural complexion'. Today, unless I am less observant than most, the opposite would almost seem to be the case. The average woman in Athens wears little daytime makeup, though evenings produce their quota of glamour.

It was the Propylaea which became the Palace of the Duke of Athens, and if you look above the north wing you can still see the joint sockets where another storey was added; the south wing is the unfinished portion. There is nothing beyond the third column, and learned opinion is that it was here that Mnesicles halted the work until he could persuade the priests to withdraw their objections. I used to like to go out on to the small L shaped foundation. There is a splendid view of the unfortunates still struggling up the steps, which is particularly satisfactory when one has just achieved the climb, drawn breath, and is ready for the next assault.

If the little temple of Athena Nike is full of sightseers, bide your time and come back later, turning instead towards the Parthenon itself. All this area must have been crammed with buildings for the past 2000 years. Certainly there have been other temples, and equally certainly there was a chapel during Frankish rule and, most important for those with any imagination (and who can be otherwise than imaginative in this place despite the crowds, the noise of a summer afternoon and the photographers all jostling for the best vantage points), it was somewhere here that the great statue of Athena Promachos stood. The helmeted giantess stood over 30 feet high, a shield on her left arm, with her right leaning on a spear. It was said that even as ships approached from as far away as Sounion, sailors could see the helmet plume and the spear flashing in the sunlight, and it is highly probable that when St Paul came this was also his first sight of Athens. Medallions and written descriptions have been invaluable in giving us a fairly full description of the statue, which is fortunate because the mighty warrior was removed to Constantinople, and in 1203 was destroyed because, said the superstitious inhabitants, the martial goddess was summoning the Crusaders to her aid. Obviously there was little difference to the Saracen between Olympian gods and the Christian one. No trace at all remains in Athens of the statue, though it is thought that two large blocks, with some moulding still visible, might possibly have been part of her plinth.

One used to be able to walk along between the tall columns of the Parthenon and into the roofless interior, to get the feeling of being near to the spot where the other, even more famous, statue of Athena stood in early times, but the destructive march of tourist hordes has been as bad as that of other invaders, so that the privilege may forever be denied.

The name Parthenon is used today for the whole building, but originally was given to the room within the structure, referred to as the 'virgin's apartment'. Experts have also expressed the opinion that it also means chamber of the maidens, and it could then have referred to priestesses and not to the goddess herself. This building, old as it is, was not the original building on the site. There had been an earlier one, which had been called the Hekatompedon ('hundred foot') and in the museum one can see the fragments fortunately handed down to us. When the marble quarries on Mount Pentelikon were opened, the decision was taken, possibly by Aristides, to commence the building of a new temple and these fragments of the Hekatompedon were incorporated in the terraces. Then the Persian wars broke out and by the time they ended the whole Acropolis again lay in ruins. If you look along the column drums in the Acropolis north wall, you will see marks of the great fires which must have raged, for when rebuilding was commenced these stones were deliberately placed there to be a constant reminder of Persian barbarity.

The new marble temple which was to rise on the site was to be dedicated to the Virgin Goddess Athena, but it was also to be used as a treasure house so that it did not supersede the holy temple of the Erechtheion. The master plan was given by Pericles into the care of Phidias as surveyor-general, and it was he who employed the great architect Iktinos, the contractor Kallikrates, and his own pupils and rivals to work on the friezes and metopes. Their combined work remains as one of the greatest masterpieces built by mankind.

There are 17 fluted columns on each side, and eight on either end, and to give an appearance of perfect symmetry, the horizontal construction is slightly curved, so that there is as much as two and a half inches difference on the inner surface. When the building was completed and brightly coloured in the manner of the day it must have been an impressive experience to approach the temple, let alone to glimpse the awesome figure of the goddess statue within. This statue of Athena Polias was entirely the work of Phidias and, although it no longer exists, we are fortunate in being able to conjure its likeness in our mind's eye from the graphic description left to us: 'The statue was on a pedestal and reached to a height of 39 feet. It was made of gold plate, fastened on to a wooden frame. The face, hands and feet were ivory, and her eyes blazed in precious stones. Her long dress was made of pure gold. So were her ornaments, and all were made so that in time of trouble they could be removed to a place of safety without injuring the body of the Statue.' They were indeed removed in 298 B.C. by Lachares, who fled the city, and 200 years later, the statue too had disappeared for ever. Fortunately there is a small copy, made by Varvakeion, in the National Archaeological Museum. It is not considered to be a good likeness because it does not entirely match up with the previous comments, but it is at least something.

There is an ironically sour note to all this glory. Due to Pericles' fall from grace, Phidias was attacked by the same political opponents and accused of stealing materials which should have gone into the Athena Parthenos statue (as Polias was later called), and he was forced into exile in 432 B.C., just as some of the figures were beginning to appear on the west pediment of the Parthenon, so that in his lifetime he never received his just approbation.

A small section of the Ionic frieze is still in position on this western sekos, though the rest has been scattered: some to the British Museum, some to the Louvre, some destroyed in the 1687 explosion, and some in the Acropolis Museum.

In toto, it depicted the great Panathenaic festival held every fourth year in honour of the goddess's birthday. This was in the month we know as August. An embroidered saffron peplos — a long scarf-like garment — was borne in state through Athens on a wheeled ship, with priests and priestesses in attendance. There were also musicians, sacrificial animals and athletes who had completed in the celebratory games for the prizes of tax-free olive oil from the sacred groves. Even in its decimated state, the frieze springs to life, and as one looks into the fragments left to us, one tends to forget that 2000 years have passed since these people moved and walked like us. . . .

It was in the 6th century A.D. that the Parthenon first became a Christian church, under the reign of the Roman Emperor Justinian. It was then dedicated to St Sophia, but it was re-dedicated to the Virgin Mother of God, and certain changes were made in the interior of the structure to form an apse for the altar. Vaults intended for the remains of the bishops were installed, and in fact these were only discovered in 1910.

During the thirteenth century, during the time of the Franks, the Parthenon changed faiths again. First to the Latin church, and then, later under the Turks, it became a mosque and the Byzantine belltower was converted to a mosque. The last foreign travellers to see the building intact were Carrey, Spon and Wheler during the seventeenth century, but fortunately Jacques Carrey made many sketches of the sculptures in 1674, which now form an invaluable collection in the Bibliothèque Nationale in Paris.

It was in 1687 while the Parthenon was being used as a powder magazine by the Turks that a shell, fired from the Mouseion Hill carried away most of the cella, the frieze and many of the columns. In addition, Morosini, on gaining entry to the Acropolis, tried to carry off the horses and chariot of Athens. It fell, and shattered. Since then, the Parthenon has been a comparatively peaceful place, surviving Nazi rule, civil war, and, for a brief period, British occupation. But the great memorial to Pericles and to the work of Phidias has by no means outlived its glory, or its usefulness. It is still the lodestone for thousands of visitors from all over the world, and even if it has suffered in the process, it has more than justified its building by the pleasure it has afforded to all who have seen it, or merely read about it.

Again and again legend enters the lists when contending for our interest in the buildings on the Acropolis and, for me, the winner must always be the Erechtheion, with its lovely southern porch whose pale, begrimed copy stands as part of a church in London's Euston Road. The story of the Erechtheion springs straight from the mists of Creation. There are many versions, but it seems that Earth and Fire (Haephestus) gave birth to a creature which was part human and part serpent, called Erichthonios. It was put into a chest and given by its fostermother Athena into the care of the three daughters of Kekrops. He later became king of Athens (though in his time it was called Kekropia), and to him is attributed the institution of the Panathenaic procession. Serpents have always played a large part on the folklore of many peoples, and there were always legends of sacred snakes guarding the Erechtheion, said to be built where the palace of the Mycaenean kings once stood.

The building is also traditionally the place where the great contest for the possession of Athens, or Kekropia, took place between Athena and Poseidon. There is an opening in the floor in the interior room, where one could see the spring of salt water supposedly started by Poseidon's trident and in the courtyard Athena's olive tree was supposed to grow. (Herodotus claimed that it magically resprouted after the fires left by the Persian sack.) There is an olive tree there today, though a bit of a fraud. It was planted on 22 February 1917 (George Washington's birthday) by one Bert Hodge Hill, and it was in celebration of the fact that Mr Hill had discovered a water pipe which, he reasoned, must have been there to take care of something special, and which, he equally reasoned, might have been *the* tree. Nevertheless, Mr Hill's tree is a pleasant modern addition to the legend.

It is also in this same place that the xoanon of Athena

Polias, a strangely shaped piece of wood said to have fallen from the sky, was housed and worshipped. Snakes, goddesses, myths, half-truths, facts, all mixed inextricably in one exquisite little building of whose statues one is held in exile in the British Museum, while her sister Caryatids are to be incarcerated for perpetuity in the Acropolis equivalent, against the ravages of wind and weather. Prisoners indeed . . . perhaps the only true moments in the whole history of the Erechtheion were during the days when this shrine to a virgin goddess was given over to the pleasures of the Turkish seraglio.

One of the most revealing views in Athens is obtained from the wall at the northern porch of the Erechtheion. Below lies the Agora, the Thesion, the Stoa of Attalus, the tiled roofs of Byzantine churches and the little houses of the Plaka. In the middle distance is the newer city, grey and white with the sun awnings striped like tigers above the balconies, and beyond, scarred by modern intrusions on its slopes, Mount Parnis, and the olive-green hills of Attica. In the heat of midsummer dust haze may obscure this fascinating glimpse of other peoples' lives, but come in moonlight, when the shabbiness is hidden and only the delicacy of the uncaring stones can be seen, soaring above the neon of the city lights, and the beauty of this place transcends everything. Then, and only then, does one understand the magical properties of the Erechtheion. . . .

One sunny day in August, I spent over half an hour trying fruitlessly to photograph the Wingless Victory, or, to call it by its proper name, the Temple of Athena Nike. There was an apparition in a striped T-shirt who inevitably popped around corners at awkward moments, so I gave up, as I advised you to do some pages ago, and went back later. Perhaps by the time you get there, the crowds will have departed and the striped T-shirt be no longer in evidence, so you can take time to look properly at this little gem of careful reconstruction. Designed by Kallicrates in the 5th century B.C. the original commemorated the victories over Persia but there were quarrels over the designs, probably instigated by the same priests whose land abutted.

The temple was destroyed by the Turks when they required the site for a gun emplacement, so when reconstruction was to be undertaken by Ross, Schaubert and Hansen in 1836-42 they resorted to the drawings, made by the invaluable Stuart and Revett, of a small temple near the Illisos stream which had also been designed by Kallicrates and was said to closely resemble the Athena Nike on the Acropolis. Just before the Second World War, the bastion upon which the reconstruction had taken place was found to be unsafe, so that the whole thing had to be demolished and rebuilt yet again. The most interesting feature of the little temple is the friezes. They depict the battle of Plateia, and give an excellent idea of the Plateians who fought at Marathon, particularly useful if you intend to go out to that legendary site, one fine afternoon. The reason for the title of Wingless Victory by which the temple was known for centuries is also interesting. Originally there was a wooden statue, presumably destroyed during the Persian battles, followed by a marble goddess with a pomegranate in one hand and a helmet in the other. The pomegranate is the symbol of fertility in classical symbolism. The name of the goddess was Athena Nike—Athena, bringer of victory. There was also a goddess Nike, who had wings, and, as usual, the two goddesses got mixed up over the years. Pausanias said that the Athenians deliberately gave no wings to their statue to prevent victory flying away. Other remnants from this pretty little temple are in the Acropolis Museum. This is another point of the Acropolis which gives a superb view, all the way to the mountains and to the sea. It was on this spot, that Aegeus, father of Theseus stood, waiting for his son's return from fighting the Minotaur, and remembering that the boy had promised, if he was successful, to hoist a white sail. But alas for promises, forgotten in the excitement of the moment of victory, Theseus kept the black sail in position, and seeing it, Aegeus threw himself from the rock. Thus, Theseus sailed home to don the mantle of kingship, and 'grieved sorely for the manner of his father's death.'

Some people bypass the Acropolis Museum considering

that they will get more than enough museum time in the National Archaelogical, and in any case prefer to see the ancient buildings and not bits of them. Consequently the museum is often the haunt of the group visitors, marshalled through whether they will or not, and of the true seeker after knowledge. Now that so much more of the treasured statuary is to be housed away from the elements the museum will see a lot more of the general flow of visitors. The collection already contains all the main items discovered since 1834 despite the fact that the museum has had to be reconstructed and has only been reopened in sections over the years.

The Parthenon frieze is the raison d'être for the Acropolis Museum. Wherever one treads in classical Athens, it is this procession whose name comes up again and again. Here in the museum one is able to get nearer to the pieces and the people hurl themselves into one's consciousness even more than on the remnants on the Parthenon. As a lover of horses, it always amuses me to see one particular section. A groom is trying, very unsuccessfully, to keep an unruly horse in order, and my mind pictures the sarcasms of the head groom as the procession is delayed.... Anyone who has had a similar experience with a wilful four legged charge will laugh — and sympathise.

If you have not had enough of ancient monuments for today, you could make your way along the lower slopes of the Acropolis to the Theatre of Dionysus. It was rebuilt by Lycurgus in the 3rd or 4th century B.C. to replace an earlier structure, and is in rather bad order. The examples of theatrical buildings at Delphi and Epidaurus are much better. But this theatre must have seen many exciting things. Bacchanalian feasts, plays by Euripides and Aristophanes, probably Sophocles too. It must have been a bit of a marathon (that word again) to sit through these dramatic spectacles, so it is no wonder they were enlivened by a certain amount of carousing. And after all, modern day critics take refuge in the bar for far shorter plays and probably with less excuse.

The present circular stage was added in Roman times, and

so too was the marble barrier which was probably erected to protect the audience from wild animal shows. Look closely at the front seats, the names of regular patrons would appear to be inscribed on them, but the best, opposite the altar, was reserved not for the emperor or the prime minister but for the priest. It has beautiful depictions of a cockfight, as well as Persians in combat with gryphons.

Above the theatre is the little chapel of Our Lady of the Cavern with its walls of faded Byzantine paintings. Every evening the chapel is lit by a solitary lamp. Long ago, it was a temple to Dionysus and had been consecrated by one Thrasyllus. Until 1827, when Turkish guns destroyed it, a choregic monument of Thrasyllus had stood, from 320 B.C. in front of the cave. Nearby, a Roman statue of Dionysus was found which now reposes in the British Museum.

Why Dionysus, or Bacchus, as the Romans called him? Long prior to the 6th century B.C. festivals between competing goat-skin clad choruses were held before altars to the gods in the countryside, where the vines flourished. These were the forerunners to the tragedies and of Greek drama as we know it. It is far too complicated a subject on which to propound here, and has no place in a general guidebook to Athens, but I would suggest that if you are interested you should delve into the excellent book written by A. W. Pickard-Cambridge on the *Theatre of Dionysus in Athens.*

There is another historic piece of hillside just above the theatre, which all too often is ignored by the casual visitor. When a plague scourged the inhabitants of the Acropolis in 429 B.C., they built an altar at a known sacred spring on the hillside, offered sacrifices and washed in the waters, then went to a building where smoke poured over them from altar incense, a process called 'incubation'. Hallucinatory dreams were also produced by the smoke and the emotions, and through this combination of circumstances, the god Asklepios, previously worshipped almost exclusively at Epidaurus (see chapter 5), was presumed to effect his cures. Attestations to the miraculous cures were legion, and took the form of votives, hung around the dormitories and sanctuaries in the vicinity of the spring. Some of these can be seen in the National Museum. Of course, when Christianity came to Athens, the miracles were immediately seen to be the work of saints, and a suitable chapel was built. The Turks had no such niceties and built fortifications in the area. Nowadays, the chapel door is locked, but I am told the spring is still there.

The roofless auditorium of the Odeion of Herodes Atticus has undergone careful reconstruction of seating and of the orchestra area. Built in the 2nd century A.D. in memory of Herodes' wife, Regilla, it is still one of the most perfect settings one can find for impressive festivals or momentous occasions.

Son et lumière, staged at the Acropolis in summer (April to October) is viewed from the Pnyx, one of the low hills which face the ancient city. This which was originally the meeting place for the Assembly, and the name, roughly translated, means 'densely crowded'. It must have been a fairly accurate description, for, as the quorum required to pass a law, 5000 citizens had to be present. These were acquired by the simple method of rounding up the citizens in a few streets within red painted cords. If someone tried to dodge he had to get by the wet red paint, which left telltale red marks which were almost indelible; anyone marked so automatically forfeited his citizen's allowance. Perhaps we should try the method with vote and responsibility dodgers today! Pericles, Themistocles, Demosthenes, all the famous names of their day must have spoken from the great basin of stone which might be called the original Speakers Corner. Don't get mixed between the Assembly, at the Pnyx, and the Council of nobles which met at the Areopagus. They were just as much in contrast as the House of Commons and the House of Lords, and, as they still do, had different purposes towards the common good.

The next little hill is Mouseion, easily distinguished by the Roman monument to Philopappus, a prince of Syria, which crowns it. There are caves and cisterns within the hill and one of them is popularly supposed to have been the prison of Socrates and where he drank the hemlock. There is no proof that this was not the place, so until such evidence comes to light, it continues to hold the name. What is accurately known is that the Mouseion was the commencing point for the Themistoclean Wall (the Long Wall) to the south, and that there was a fort on this point in the 3rd century. It was also from here that the Venetians bombarded the Acropolis in 1687. More recently, as everyone in Athens knows, some of the activities connected with the coup of 1967 took place on the Mouseion.

Less well known is the Hill of the Nymphs, where the Observatory and the radio station now stand. This is considered by many experts to have been the Athenian place of execution, but more certain is the trace of the Northern Long Wall, as well as a little Pnyx.

The first time I went to the Agora was via the entrance over the railway bridge from Adrianou. It was a bitter January day and I was glad to take refuge in the Stoa of Attalus so carefully reconstructed with monies raised in the ever generous United States of America, but even there the wind whistled hollowly between the polished and deserted colonnades, and it was difficult to conjure the necessary pictures of Athenians working, walking, and ever gossiping as Athenians have never ceased to do. On special occasions, they would have used the building to watch the Panatheniac procession winding its way past en route to the Acropolis, but it was originally erected by Attalus the Second, king of Pergamon in the 2nd century B.C. as a shopping arcade, and indeed, if one compares it with the modern equivalents found in cities throughout the Western world, it is not dissimilar.

After sterling service for about 400 years, the Stoa was destroyed (I cannot imagine our supermarkets lasting that long) but fortunately part of it survived when it was incorporated into the Valerian Wall, so that it is possible to know exactly what it looked like in its heyday. It dominates the eastern boundary of the Agora, taking one's eyes away from the area which was completely cleared of the houses erected through the intervening centuries, and even from the little sites which lie along the railway line, and which were discovered when that was built. The miserable little houses, mostly from Turkish times, might have been interesting to us too . . . but now it is the Agora which continues to be revealed, though it will take many years of patient work to complete it. This is one site in Athens where it pays to employ an official guide to escort you around if time is short. Otherwise, arm yourself with the splendid guidebooks available at the ticket office and set forth.

It might be an idea to go to the Agora Museum, housed in the Stoa, first, for without some idea of what you are looking for it is rather like unravelling Hampton Court Maze. I can only point you at the main things which you really should not miss. Three large figures stand in the centre of the Agora. These are known as the Giants, but you will see that two have fish tails instead of legs, and therefore represent Tritons. There were six of these mammoths, and they formed part of the second Odeion, destroyed in the ravages of the Goths in 267 A.D. Also in this area was the Gymnasium, in use as the principal seat of learning until Justinian closed the schools in Athens in 529 A.D. The Magistrates House, the Tholos, the Metreon which housed all city records, the Great Drain which runs straight in front of the Metreon foundations and those of the Stoa of Zeus, can all come gradually into focus. The altar performed the function of a measuring point, much as Charing Cross and Hyde Park Corner do in London, but it was also a sanctuary stone at one time. Socrates probably knew this area very well and it was likely that he spent some of his days within the Stoa of Zeus, discussing his theories, although it is also known that he visited the shop of the cobbler Simon, thought to have been somewhere near the junctions of the Great Drain. Certainly the Stoa was the venue for the court of Ostracism. So far, this Stoa is only partially uncovered, for during the building of the railway in 1891, the north wing was destroyed, though fragments may be seen in the Agora Museum. You can actually find the boundary stone of the Agora. Called the Horos, it marked the point beyond which convicted persons were not permitted to pass.

You may have noticed that when looking down on the Agora from the Acropolis wall, it is the Thesion, or Thission, which catches the eye. It deserves attention, for on closer inspection it is almost perfect, and in my opinion is one of the prettiest buildings in Athens. But it remains rather neglected in the sightseers' books, probably because of its setting. Yet, where else should it be? It was, originally, dedicated to Haephestus, god of Fire and blacksmiths, and the mean streets close by are still given over to that trade, as well as leatherworkers and electricians. It stands just a little above them on a slight slope, and gives an excellent idea of what the Parthenon must have looked like to our ancestors, although it is smaller and slightly older. There is little to see inside, apart from a few memorials, a piece of graffiti by Byron(—strange how he had a penchant for inscription. He succeeded in defacing the Temple at Sounion as well) and the friezes. They depict the story of Theseus and that is how the present name, for which I have given two of its various spellings, came into being.

It is quite remarkable that this little temple was allowed to survive so long, for it too underwent various changes. It was converted into a church and underwent some surgery in the process while being renamed St George. Under Turkish rule, the liturgy was allowed to be sung there once a year, so among local people St George was nicknamed the 'Idler'. It had a brief period of glory when used for the services at King Otto's accession in 1834, and again for a centenary service commemorating that event. Nowadays one sees few people there, although it is a delightful spot, with its pleasant little flower gardens, its uninterrupted view of the Acropolis walls on the stark rock, and of the little church which seeks shelter below them.

This little church is the Church of the Holy Apostles and, as it was built between 1000 and 1025, is probably one of the first important churches in Athens. It was restored by the American School of Classical Studies to a state resembling the original. We should remember that it was built upon the ruins of a semi-circular fountain of the 2nd century A.D.

but there was an even older fountain behind it, traces of which still remain. It is dated 6th century B.C., so perhaps the later one stood for a time in its place. While in the Agora Museum, you may have had time to look at some of the beautiful Athenian coins on display there. Some of these were made in the Argyrokopeion—the Mint—and this also stood near the old fountain.

If you leave the Agora by Adrianou, instead of using one of the other two exits, you could stop off for a drink in one of the innumerable cafes before venturing to the Kerameikos. You might need it, for the area you will be visiting is one of the most unedifying. Yet it is important, and should not really be left out unless very pressed for time, for here you will find the point where all the roads to Athens converged in ancient times. This was the gate called Dipylon, which led into the Dromos, and thence to the Agora. Dipylon means 'two gates', and consisted then of an outer and an inner portal. Between them was the traditional haunt of prostitutes, waiting to greet the travellers with their services. At the Dipylon there is still part of one of the gate towers, and a bit of *the* Wall.

The Kerameikos lay outside the Wall, and although it was known that it had to be somewhere in the vicinity, it only came to light in the late nineteenth century. Work has proceeded very slowly and much remains to be done. The most notable feature is the Street of the Tombs, because it was here that Pericles delivered the immortal oration on the Heroes of the Pelopponese. The Oberlaender Museum is worth a visit, but most of the best funerary *steles* are now ensconced in the National Museum, so unless you are an absolutely dedicated sightseer, an avid lover of tomb inscriptions, or intending to write school essays, you can save your feet that little extra bit of work by seeing the pieces in the National. On a winter visit, when the wind is cold, I'd certainly advise it. In summer, it would be worth braving the heat and the noise.

And, before leaving this area, two more pieces of information might be usefully absorbed. The ruins of the Sacred Gate are near the Kerameikos, the starting point of the

Panathenaic procession. Further out, along the north side of the Corinth Road, is the sacred olive grove once known as the Academy of Plato. The trees were said to be cuttings from the Acropolis tree given by Athena. Before going all the way out there, check at the Tourist Information Bureau. Times at many of the main sites do vary, particularly seasonally, and especially so with preservation work being undertaken. Up-to-date literature can be obtained in a positive flood from the Greek National Tourist Offices in cities all over the world, so take advantage of their very efficient organisation.

There must be many visitors to Athens (and I must admit that for a long time I was one of them) who do little more than give Hadrian's Arch a passing glance while hurtling past along Amalia Avenue in bus, taxi or car, and even fewer who actually set foot inside the precincts of the Temple of Olympian Zeus, probably because to get into the site you have to walk round to Leoforas Olgas (Olgas Avenue) though both places are very useful landmarks for the newcomer. Another reason for this apparent neglect is that both have Roman overtones, and although, almost anywhere else other than Athens, they would be hailed as magnificent relics of their age, in this city they are almost ignored. But it must not be forgotten that the Romans had great respect for the glories of Athens, and in their own way did a great deal to maintain and beautify the city, as well as excusing the Athenians many things that, committed in any other part of the great Roman Empire, would have brought down retribution.

Hadrian's Arch was built in Pentelic marble on the instructions of the Emperor Hadrian somewhere around 132 A.D. to delineate the boundaries between ancient Athens and his own new city. On one side, facing the Acropolis, it says simply, 'This is Athens, ancient city of Theseus'. On the other, it remarks, a little boastfully perhaps, 'This is the city of Hadrian and not of Theseus'. Within 'Hadrian's City' (of which incidentally more was discovered when building the Zappeion Gardens in King Otto's time) there are bits of the

Themistoclean wall, old 4th century B.C. houses and a little further over is the old watercourse of the Illisson. But naturally the Temple holds most interest. It must also hold some sort of record for building time, for though it was commenced about four centuries before the birth of Christ, work was interrupted so frequently for various reasons that it was not until 130 A.D., during Hadrian's reign, 700 years after its commencement, that it was finally ready for use. The largest temple in Greece, though not of the then known world, it originally possessed 104 great columns, but, like the ten green bottles in the song, they disappeared, each in turn. Some were destroyed by Goths, wind and weather dealt with others, and a Turkish governor removed one to be used in the construction of the Mosque of Tzistarakis, for which he was sternly rebuked from Constantinople. One column fell in 1852, and when cholera swept Athens in 1854, it was attributed to this fall, for it was belived that the ancients buried the victims of various epidemics under the columns, and the fall had opened a kind of 'Pandora's box'. Now only 16 are left. Two are seen when approaching from Leoforos Singrou, the road which contains the Olympic Airways terminal, and to me at least, these columns announce that one is, at last, within reach of the City of Theseus.

Hadrian was present at the Temple's dedication and added greatly to its glorification by presenting several statues. One was an impressive copy of the statue of Olympian Zeus executed by no less than Pheidas, a statue of Hadrian himself, and, so gossip says, one of his favourites, Antinous, who, after his death, was deified. If you are curious to know what this youth looked like, and happen to be at Delphi, there is a statue of him there, in the Museum. It shows he had undeniable good looks.

When coming out of the Temple site, take your courage in your hands and dash across the traffic to the Stadium. Now completely restored, it was built in 330 B.C. by Lycurgus for the athletic contests associated with the Panathenaic festivals, and was completely reseated in 194 A.D. by the same Herodes Atticus who donated the theatre on the side of the

Acropolis hill. The tunnel used in Roman times, probably for the exit and entry of animals and men in blood sports, can still be seen. At one time it degenerated into a quarry, but after excavations in 1869 by Ziller, interest revived and, when the Olympic Games were resuscitated in 1869, George Averoff, a wealthy benefactor, completely re-equipped the Stadium to seat 60,000. I find it a rather lonely little place, tucked away on the far side of 'Hadrian's City', but it has undeniable elegance.

It is on this side of Olympian Zeus's Temple that one is nearer the banks of the Illisson, where Plato and other philosophers are reputed to have walked. Mostly covered and out of sight now, there is little to see but it is just such snippets of information which stimulate the imagination.

3 Son et Lumière-
Modern Athens

The days begin very early for me in Athens, whatever the season. I love the lemon and honey light which casts its spell over the most mundane apartment blocks, before the dust rises from the mounting traffic and when the air is still cool and sweet. In summer, as I sip my coffee on the little balcony, I look across the narrow canyon between the houses. A caged canary who lives out his days on the shadowed wall of the balcony opposite has not been put out for his daily airing, for his owners, like the rest of the Mediterranean peoples, seldom open the shutters to daylight, and the building has an eyeless appearance. In the street below, a little black-shawled lady shuffles unhurriedly towards the corner, past the overflowing refuse bins awaiting collection, and the rows of cars. Athens usually leaves its vehicles at odd angles at night, with wheels perched drunkenly on the kerbstones, so that the morning presents a decidedly hungover appearance, and the cars are as big a hazard to pedestrians as their erratic drivers are later in the day.

If I lean out, I can just glimpse the road that leads across to the Zappeion Gardens, and already the decibels are rising. Sleep is no longer possible, though these side streets are surprisingly quiet. One could almost be in a village (and Athens strikes me as a series of villages)—I can even hear the contented cluck of hens somewhere in the tiny gardens at the back of the flats. The small shops and tavernas in the residential areas bear a great resemblance to their cousins in country districts, and have even got the same ragged fringe of elderly men dressed in respectable dark suits,

whose tobacco exudes the familiar country acridity, and on
the little sortie to collect fresh milk and coarse new bread one
gets similar courteous acknowledgements to the morning
greetings. I feel that I've lived here always. Can it only be a
week or two since I came. . . ?

What to do on this new day? Inevitably comes the same
temptation. There is still much to see when it looks as if the
day is going to be fine. Thank goodness it so often is, but
although I never tire of the classical sites, I do have an
inbuilt objection to spending sunlit hours indoors and must
find something to do which keeps me out under the blue sky.

But it isn't always fine. In winter, when the wind and the
rain can be very temperamental, is the time to make for the
museums until the weathercocks change direction. Check in
This Week in Athens, or the *Athenian* for the opening times of
various premises. They too can follow the climate's example
and be temperamental, requiring certain days for cleaning etc.
As a rough guide, one can say that they are open mornings
and afternoons in summer, and mornings only in winter.
Some of the classical museums, such as the ones at the
Acropolis, Kerameikos and Agora, are part of an outdoor
site, and one can be covered when visiting them; in summer
they can afford a welcome breather from the hot sunshine.
But others are situated in the modern city, and are also an
essential part of a knowledge of Athens, and if you are
limited to one brief period in the Greek capital, then the
sacrifice of precious sunlight hours has to be paid. Most
museums open on Sundays, which is useful, and are often
free on that day and on Thursdays. Fees vary. On payment of
an extra fee, photography with a small camera is allowed at
some museums, but if you intend to set up tripods and other
gadgetry, prior arrangements must be made.

But however enticing the weather, there is one museum
to which I never mind going. The National Archaeological
Museum, on Patission, ranks, in my opinion as one of the
most interesting and essential ingredients in any visit to
Athens, as well as being universally recognised as one of the
greatest museums in the world. It would be impossible to do

more than give you an idea of the pieces which must not be missed in the pages of this book. After all, volumes have been devoted to the collections to be found there. Also, although items are often labelled clearly in several languages you will require a full catalogue (obtainable at the entrance) because, as in any museum, there is a constant programme of painting, refurnishing etc, and things get moved around. Apart from that, I have only one piece of advice to give — do not try to hurry. This museum is the key, not just to Athens, but to Greece. Learn to use it properly and it will open the door to the sites you visit in that lovely land.

Almost the first thing to greet your eye is the golden death-mask of a Mycenean king, discovered by Schliemann in Grave Circle A at Mycenae, and known as the Mask of Agememnon. Although later scientific investigation into dating has proved this to be unlikely, the title remains, and to date there is no other claimant. The Mycenean room is a glowing mass of gold, ivory, silver and jewelled ornaments which were found in incredible array in the grave circles and elsewhere on sites at Tiryns, Pylos and Mycenae. These peoples, who lived thousands of years before Christ, believed in an after life, and 'grave goods' helped them along their journey to the next world. It is fortunate for us that they did believe in this way, for it made them bury many beautiful things with their highborn dead and in so doing have bequeathed a priceless and complete picture of their everyday life. You may want to come several times to the Mycenae room. Most visitors come once, and then, after having visited the sites themselves, come back and look again.

The golden Vapheio Cups, which came Vapheio in Laconia and are Minoan in design, are exquisite. They show the influences of the Crete-Mycenean world, one depicting a bull caught in a net, another bull turning at bay towards its hunters, and yet another running as fast as he can. Another cup shows an ingenious method of bull catching using a heifer as bait. Equally beautiful is a rhyton, used for pouring the libation to the gods, formed in the shape of a bull's head, while another favourite, although in a different category entirely, is the bowl of crystal rock with a duck's head. There are bronze daggers inlaid with gold and silver, showing a lion hunt in progress, and bracelets and rings depict religious scenes which bring the classical world alive for us. None of these items would be out of place in today's world, so classic is the workmanship, and, quite naturally, modern designers still turn to these items for inspiration. It is possible to buy modern copies of the Vapheio Cups in certain jewellers in Athens. Expensive—but after all, they too have a precious uniqueness.

In another room of the museum one can find a Roman copy of the Parthenon Athena by Phidias. It is not a particularly good copy, according to the experts, because there are, apparently, discrepancies between it and the description left by the ubiquitous Pausanias. But at least it gives some idea of the awesomeness of the real thing. The precious stone eyes seem to blaze out from the ivory face and the pure golden dress must have gleamed in the dusk until the eyes of the beholder could have sworn that she moved.

The bronzes, many of which have been dredged from the seabed, are particularly fine—especially the little jockey of Artemision. How light he seems as he gallops his invisible horse for eternity. He was probably being transferred to Constantinople when the ship on which he was travelling foundered off Cape Artemision. Another graceful boy is the youth of Marathon. What did his hands hold? Did Poseidon take the offering as this youth, too, sank below the waves? We shall never know. But closer acquaintance with the characters of these gods of Ancient Greece, as they are related to us, leads me to think that Poseidon's much-vaunted vanity could not have possibly allowed him to let us have these treasures back from his kingdom without sending the finest of all . . . a statue of himself. It has a majesty, a sense of virility, and, too, a faint sense of foreboding, which is not entirely due only to empty eye sockets. Perhaps it is the most becoming green patina with which long immersion in his natural element has endowed him. After all, if, as experts think, this statue was originally carved after the victory at Salamis, he's been going strong for 2000 years.

Among the marbles, which are legion, look particularly for the trio which one highly respected American guidebook calls the 'The Slipper Slapper'. It is a most accurate description, and cannot be bettered. Aphrodite has been caught in the nude by the importunate Pan, while Cupid laughs to see such fun. . . . Very different, and sufficient to remind that sorrow is not just the prerogative of the living today, is the funerary *stele* from the Kerameikos. It shows a touching farewell between a young girl and her mother, while her father looks on with longing and with love. There is also the Apollo, found in 1959 in Piraeus when workmen were digging the foundations for a sewer, the bronze Athena, also from Piraeus, and the bronze of Athena Promachos from the Acropolis, and many, many more. Even if you are not particularly interested in statuary in the normal way, these deserve your undivided attention, despite the pull of so many other Athenian attractions. If you like unusual and beautiful jewellery, however, do go up to see the priceless Stathatou collection, which was given complete to the nation and is housed as such.

The growing interest in numismatics, may be among your hobbies too. If so, a marvellous selection of over 300,000 coins can be seen in another section of the National Archaelogical Museum. (The price of admission is included in the ticket for the main museum.) Space is rather limited in the tourist car parks at the museum, particularly when the coaches arrive, and with a locally registered car you might not get in. I usually circle round and into the nearby street called Tossitsa, or into the narrow streets at the back of the museum area. It is a little easier to come to the museum by taxi or bus, or if your hotel is in the Omonia area it is no distance to walk.

'My wish is that even after my death, something of myself should remain in the museum which I created with such enthusiasm and love. I therefore direct that my heart shall be immured in the entrance.' These are the sentiments inscribed at the beginning of the guidebook to the Benaki

Museum. They were those of the founder, Antony Benaki. I had never visited the museum and felt a bit guilty about constantly ignoring it, but the fact is that one walks so many times along Vassileos Sofias and never notices the building other than as a rather elegant house set among a dozen others of the same ilk, some of which are now the embassies. So, one November morning, when it had rained rather hard and the sky held promise of more libations from the gods, three of us walked down from the Hilton Hotel with the express intention of 'doing' the Benaki at last. It took three passers-by and two policemen before we discovered it, and it showed me that Athenians, just as much as Londoners, have no idea where the treasurehouses of their city are situated. For this is indeed a treasurehouse. The mansion, situated at the corner of Vassileos Sofias and Odos Koumbari, was formerly the home of Emmanual Benaki, and it was his children and his grand-daughter who gave the building to the Greek nation for the purpose of housing the priceless historical and artistic collections that Antony Benaki had assembled over a period of 35 years. The aim was to provide a warm living atmosphere, rather than a dull museum building, and, from its inception, Anthony Benaki supervised the presentation of exhibits, arranging many as we see them today. When he died in 1954, he further bequeathed a large sum for its maintenance, a generosity which has been followed by many donations, both from his family and from other people, and which supplement the State contributions for regular expenses.

It has to be emphasised that this collection was, in the beginning, dictated according to the founder's tastes and interests, and is not entirely Greek in content. But there are many items of particular interest to the foreigner anxious to learn a little more about the country he is visiting. There is, for example, a most attractive collection of ancient Greek jewellery as well as more modern pieces (for example, an exquisite caravel pendant from Patmos). There is too a superb assembly of national costumes which show the variety of styles and designs which have developed over the years, and there is an impressive selection of religious objects, including crosses, mitres, chalices, embroidered screens and magnificent ikons—particularly important, for it must be remembered that ikons were a most important manifestation of Greek art and thought during the long period of Turkish rule. One sees that, throughout, despite a small amount of Italian influence, the whole leaning is towards Byzantine art forms. It is interesting, (particularly in view of the fact that Crete was, until the 1660s, the foremost centre of artistic development in the area) to see the early works of El Greco (Domenicos Theotokopoulos) in this collection, for he was of course, born in the little village of Fodhele in Crete. One is a portable ikon in Cretan style, portraying Luke the Evangelist, which is thought to be the only work by El Greco in this form. The other is the Adoration of the Magi, which clearly shows Italian influence. Copies of these works, and of other ikons in the collection, can be bought in the museum at very reasonable cost, and make excellent souvenirs.

But possibly the most fascinating exhibits are the many relics of the War of Independence, and the fine collection of lithographs and paintings by artists of the period which give a very clear impression of what Athens looked like then, viewed from various vantage points. It is quite difficult to judge exactly where these vantage points must have been, so much has changed in a mere 150 years, but it is an interesting and time-consuming exercise.

Among the many interesting items in the room devoted to the period of the War of Independence (1821-28) and of other periods of Greek modern history, is the little writing desk that belonged to Byron. Perhaps it was upon this that he wrote of Teresa Makris, the 'Maid of Athens'? In a nearby case there is a cap, and other small possessions which once belonged to her. There are medals, portraits, the arms of various notable families, including the sword and pistol of the Cretan hero, Daskaloyannis, who was tortured to death in 1770, and the small personal relics of the famous Kapodistrias, Governor of Greece in the formative years of 1827-31, and perhaps more poignant, the last will of Karaiskakis, dated just hours before his death in 1827. It seems a pity, in a way, that all the War of

Independence souvenirs are not together in one museum, but the others are all in the National and Historical Museum of Stadion, and more of this anon.

If the ikons too have inspired further interest in the Greek religion, a visit to the Byzantine Museum might also be in order. It is not far to walk — just across the busy road from the Benaki and housed in a rather pleasant building which was built in Florentine style for the Duchesse de Plaisance in 1848. There are so many beautiful ikons and sculptures in this collection that it is honestly a matter of taste as to preference, and it is not helped by the lack of titling on exhibits, none of it in English at the time of my visit. Ask to be shown the fourteenth-century embroidery called Epistaphios of Thessaloniki, which depicts the body of Christ on a bier. This museum is closed on Monday. I do wish that the Athens museums had some cohesion on this! The best advice I can offer is to avoid most museums on Mondays *and* Tuesdays, whether it rains or not. . . .

The War Museum, a few doors further along, will either delight or horrify. Originally planned during the reign of the Colonels, it is none the less an impressive and well-planned display of Greek military history, from the time of the triremes used in the Persian Wars until the present day. The aircraft and other modern instruments of war which stand in the grounds are useful too, if for no other reason than to provide climbing blocks for every boy in Athens, from 9 to 90.

Do not confuse this museum with the National and Historical Museum in Kolokotronis Square, off Stadiou, which also houses warlike objects, though mainly in connection with the years of Turkish Occupation and of the War of Independence. The labelling, at the time of my visit at least, was in Greek only, which does present a certain difficulty for foreigners, but it is possible to get English translation copies for use in the museum, (though they cannot be taken away). Not many people other than Greek nationals and school parties go there. A pity I think, because it is an object lesson in the ephemeral glories of militarism, as it applied to the Turkish empire at least. For Philhellenes (and who isn't when visiting Greece?) it has several very interesting items, including Byron's sword and a lock of his hair. Nothing is particularly well displayed, which is surprising in this city which excels in museum presentation. The building itself is almost as interesting as its content. From Otto's time it was the parliament building and, in the stormy manner of Greek politics, a prime minister, Theodorus Delyannis, was assassinated on its steps. The statue bravely facing the traffic is one of Kolokotronis, and is a copy of the one at Nauplion, capital of the new Greek nation for a brief period after the Revolution.

Museums house the past, but emerging from the shadows of yesterday into the racket of the one-way traffic of Stadiou brings us sharply back into the apparant chaos of modern Athens. This always seems to be the impression for the first-time visitor, but it is not as difficult as it looks at first glance, particularly if armed with a map. If you haven't one, visit the Tourist Office, a bookseller, or rummage among the jumble of worry beads, chewing gum, aspirins, cigarettes and magazines found at the many *periptero,* a much nicer name than kiosk. Incidentally, you may also telephone from a *periptero,* if you can find a telephone free. Half Athens spends its time on these street telephones, talking to the other half. The periptero keepers must hear some very illuminating conversations, for I'm quite sure that all the business of the city is conducted here. . . .

Even with a map clutched firmly in hand, you may not be much wiser for, quite logically, everything is written in Greek. Nowadays many street names appear in Latinised letters as well, but signs are usually high on walls, and present yet another hazard when driving. It is often much easier on foot, and the modern Athens you are likely to want to see is not that large to cover. It is within the frame-work of the city laid down by Cleanthes and Schaubert. Syntagma Square and Omonia Square are the two main centres of tourist activities, and are reached, one from the other, by Stadiou and Venizelos. The latter is also known as

Panepistimiou, Omonia is Piccadilly with Near Eastern overtones with touts, hotdog stalls, and underground station and
shopping precinct, fountains and even flowersellers. A
lot of package hotels are in this vicinity, and therefore are
sometimes noisy.

Along Venizelos you will spot a trio of Pentelic marble
buildings which give the appearance of antiquity, but they
are in fact part of the nineteenth-century rebuilding scheme,
and house the Academy, the University and the Library.
None are vitally interesting to the casual visitor, apart from
the fact that since the fall of the junta, one inevitably finds
student meetings, soapbox orators and agitators all holding
forth on every known subject nearby. The favourite at one
time was anti-Americanism, but that novelty has worn a
little thin now. It is all part of the Athenian scene and very
entertaining. Even normal conversations in Greek sound as
if there's a gigantic row going on, so discussion of this sort
is fun to watch. At Easter, the scent from the orange blossom
on the little trees gracing the gardens around the statuary of
Athene and Apollo is delightful. I was busily engaged in
enjoying it one day, as I strolled along in the sunlight, when
I spotted a statue of Gladstone staring stonily at me. I discovered on enquiry that he earned his place on the University
forecourt because he happened to be in office at the time of
the unification of the Ionian islands with Greece. Statues
have, after all, been awarded for less . . . and to be fair, he was
a Philhellene.

It is rather interesting to note that in the artistic fields of
the sculptors and painters, no Greek name, other than El
Greco, comes to mind between the Classical era and the
formation of the independent Greek nation, although there
must have been many talented people working all over
Europe as well as perhaps within the stricter confines of the
various conquerors' domains, during those 2000 years. I have
mentioned that the religious objects were instrumental in
keeping a purer form of the Greek Orthodox Church and
they were also invaluable in allowing some expressions of
talent, but the names of the artists so employed are lost

forever. However, after 1830 there was a tremendous upsurge of work by Greek artists, and particularly by Greek sculptors, no doubt anxious to prove that the ancient crafts had not been lost with liberty for all those centuries. Some of the sculptors have achieved international importance; others have become famous only within their own country, but their work decorates many places in Greece, particularly Athens, for capital cities tend to acquire statuary as schoolboys collect stamps. But because we are usually only intent on seeing classical remains, the modern offerings get ignored in the same fashion that we walk by statues every day in our own cities and never even know who they depict. Yet behind many of them are stories just as fascinating as the classical legends.

Those which occupy space beside Gladstone and Kapodistrias outside the University are a case in point. There is Kossos's statue of Rigas Ferraios who, when he was little more than a boy, killed a Turk and was forced to flee from his home. After many wanderings, both within Greece and in Europe, he arrived in Vienna in 1796, where he began publishing poems advocating Independence for Greece and even went as far as circulating a draft constitution. The Austrians arrested him and handed him over to the Pasha of Belgrade (for at that time, Austria and Turkey ruled the present Yugoslavian provinces). Ferraios was executed by strangulation in Belgrade goal in 1797, aged 40.

Nearby stands Gregory the Fifth. A patriot all of his life, he was Patriarch of Constantinople and an indefatigable worker for Greek Independence when, on Easter Day 20 April 1821, just two weeks after the beginning of the War of Independence, the Turks arrested and hung him. The body was thrown into the sea, but was picked up by a Greek ship going to Russia, and 50 years later, in 1871, his remains were brought back to Greece and buried in the Cathedral of Athens. The statue is by Fytalis, and it shows what a wealth of material was at the disposal of this new breed of sculptors during the latter years of the nineteenth century.

Statues are so numerous in Athens that it would take too

long to mention all the important ones, let alone the lesser tributes, whether on historic or artistic grounds, but if you are interested, seek out the little book written in 1966 by J. G. Manolikakis, *The Sculpture of Modern Athens.*

Nearer to Syntagma Square, almost opposite Flocas, the expensive patisserie patronised by well-to-do Athenians and many tourists, is a rather pleasant, squarish house, side-facing the street and approached by a small iron gate. This is the Palace of Ilium (unfortunately not open to the public), once the home of the famous Schliemann, whose name must forever be linked with the discovery of the Mycenic treasures, and who persisted in his complete faith that the stories of Homer were historic fact rather than legend. His final resting-place, not far away, is in the Proto Nekrotafio, the First Cemetery of Athens, not far from the Temple of Olympian Zeus, within a mausoleum covered with impressive bas-reliefs in the Troy style, and he sleeps in good company, with Koloktronis, Makriyannis, Benaki and the George Averoff who, instead of excavating, made his contribution to the classical era of Greece by completely restoring the Olympic Stadium. This First Cemetery is usually neglected by most tourists, but if you are interested in the monuments and tombs of many who contributed to the cultural and political history of Greece in the immediate past, it is worth a visit.

I can never afford to do my shopping in the slightly elevated atmosphere of Stadiou and Venizelos in the vicinity of Syntagma, invariably ending up in the lower priced areas of Mitreopolis, or in Pangrati, but it is pleasant to window shop. Here, as elsewhere in Athens, the Mediterranean custom of closing every afternoon, is in force. It is always a little irritating at first, to witness the almost indecent haste in which shops close with a decided clang for siesta, but after a week or two, if one is wise, the routine becomes as much a habit for the visitor as for the locals. If it is not followed, it is not possible to enjoy the equally Mediterranean custom of dining late and staying up even later, when the cool summer air is so very delicious. But I am equally certain that the

1 & 2 The Acropolis: *above* the Parthenon; *below* the caryatids of the Erechtheion

3 *Opposite* The Tower of the Winds

4 *Above* Kapnikarea Church; 5 *below* the Temple of Zeus Olympus with the Acropolis in the background

6 *Above* the east end of the Little Metropolitan Cathedral;   7 *below* carvings
behind the stage of the Theatre of Dionysius

8 The Church of the Holy Apostles

9   Athens from the Acropolis, looking towards Lycabettus Hill

10   *Opposite* Easter in Athens: a charity collector with a symbolic sheep

0316-01
40 à 6x10
Taschentücher
Fazzoletti
Pañuelos
40 à 6x10

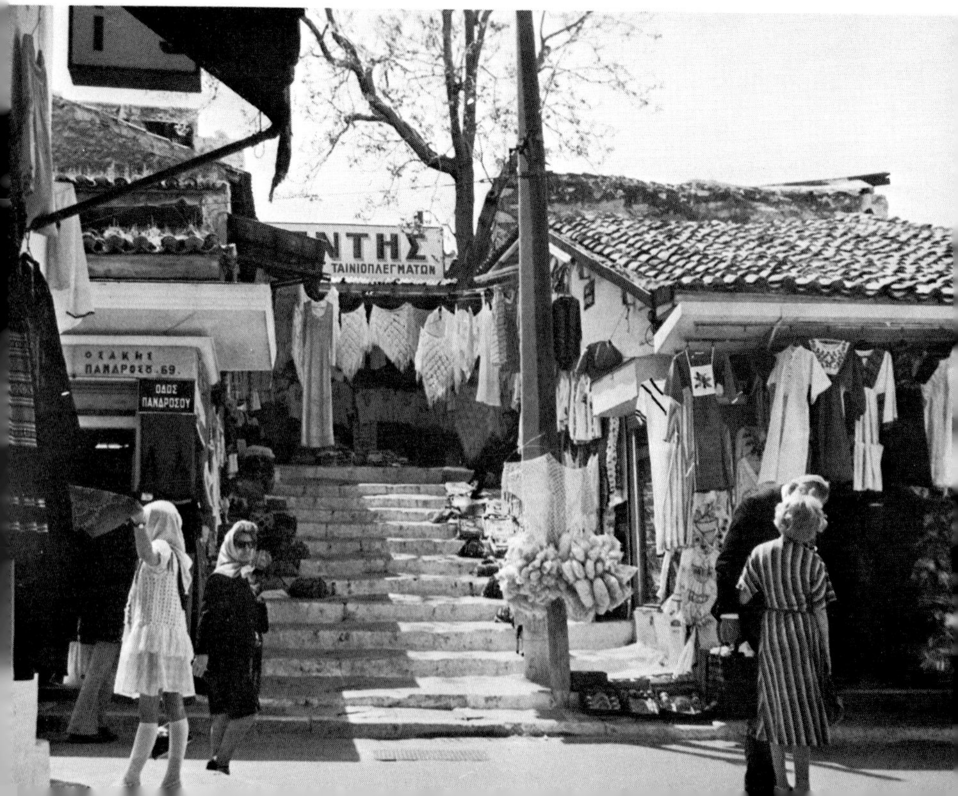
ΝΤΗΣ
ΤΑΙΝΙΟΠΛΕΓΜΑΤΩΝ
ΟΔΟΣ
ΠΑΝΔΡΟΣΟΥ

11 & 12 *Opposite* Shopping in Athens: *above* Easter bread on sale; *below* in the Plaka

13 Evzones on guard outside the Palace

14 & 15   Luck or faith; *above* lottery tickets on sale; *below* ikons

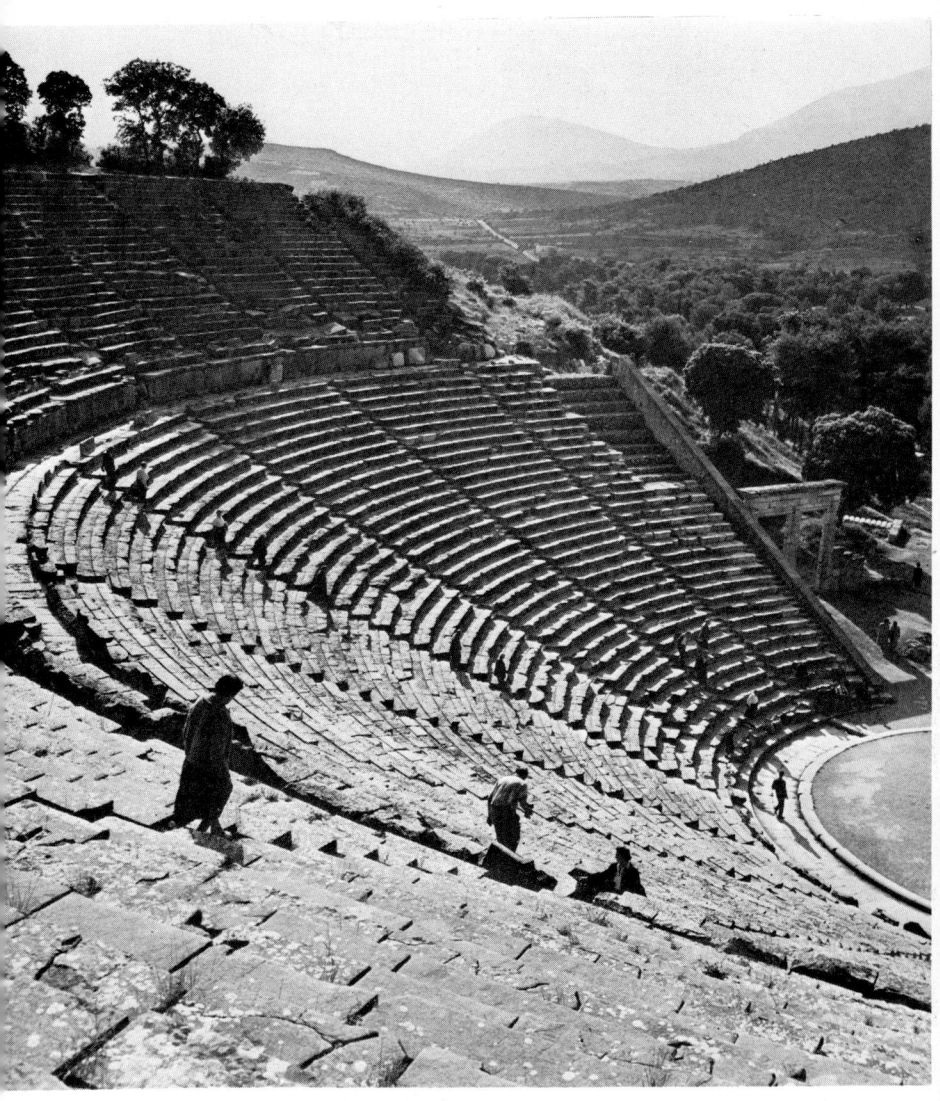

16   The theatre at Epidauros, the best preserved and most perfect of its kind

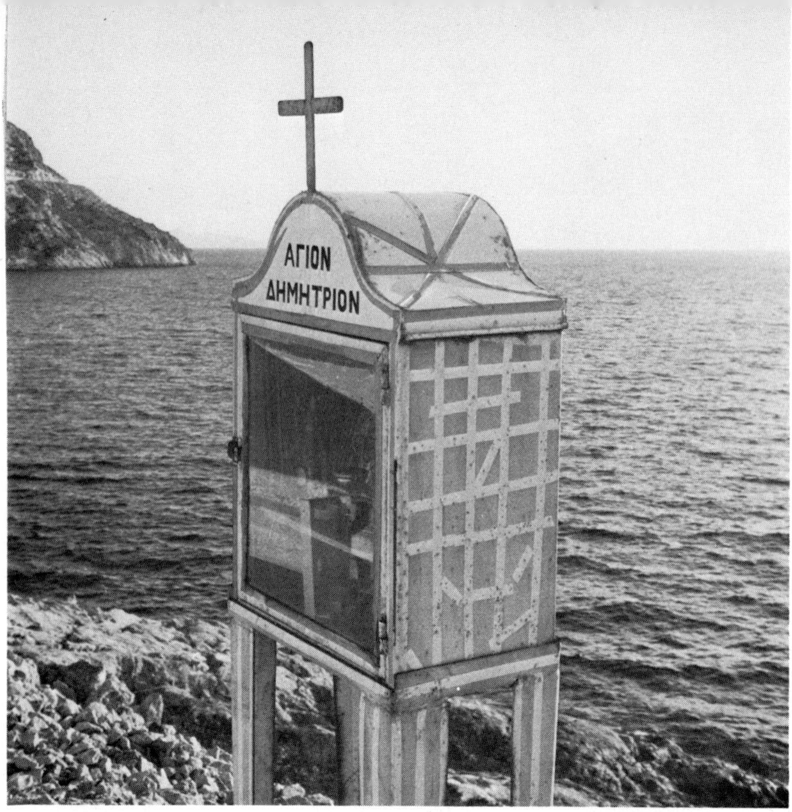
ΑΓΙΟΝ
ΔΗΜΗΤΡΙΟΝ

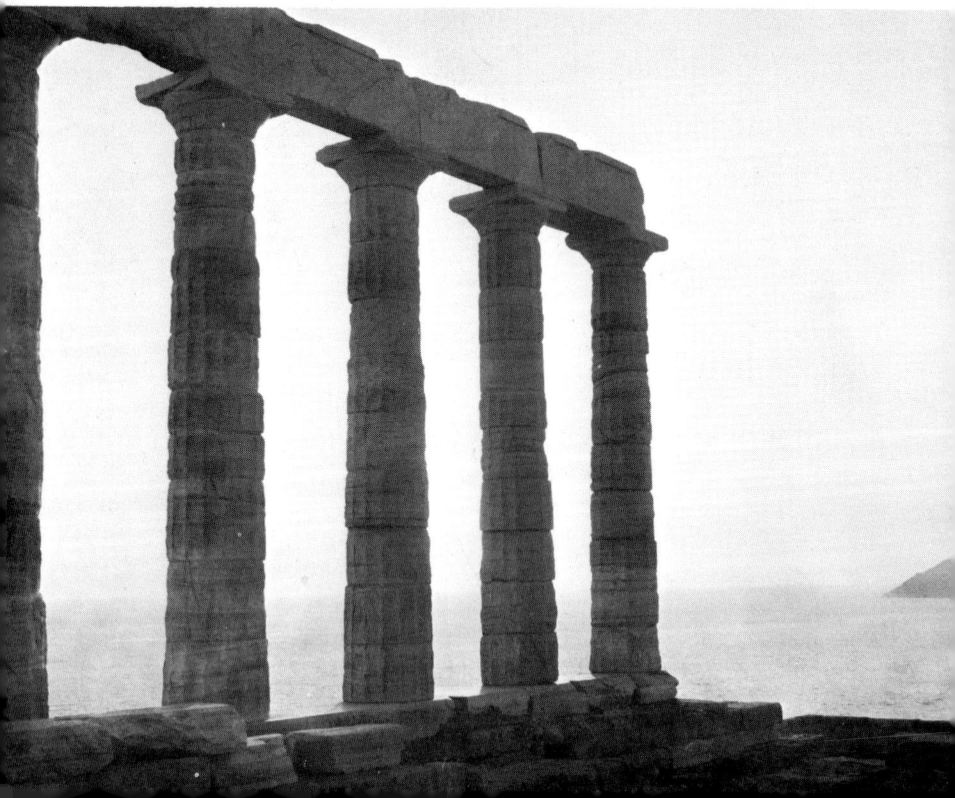

17 & 18 *Opposite* Sounion: *above* a wayside shrine; *below* the Temple of Poseidon

19 *Above* Dafni monastery; 20 *below* the small Byzantine church at Aegustina

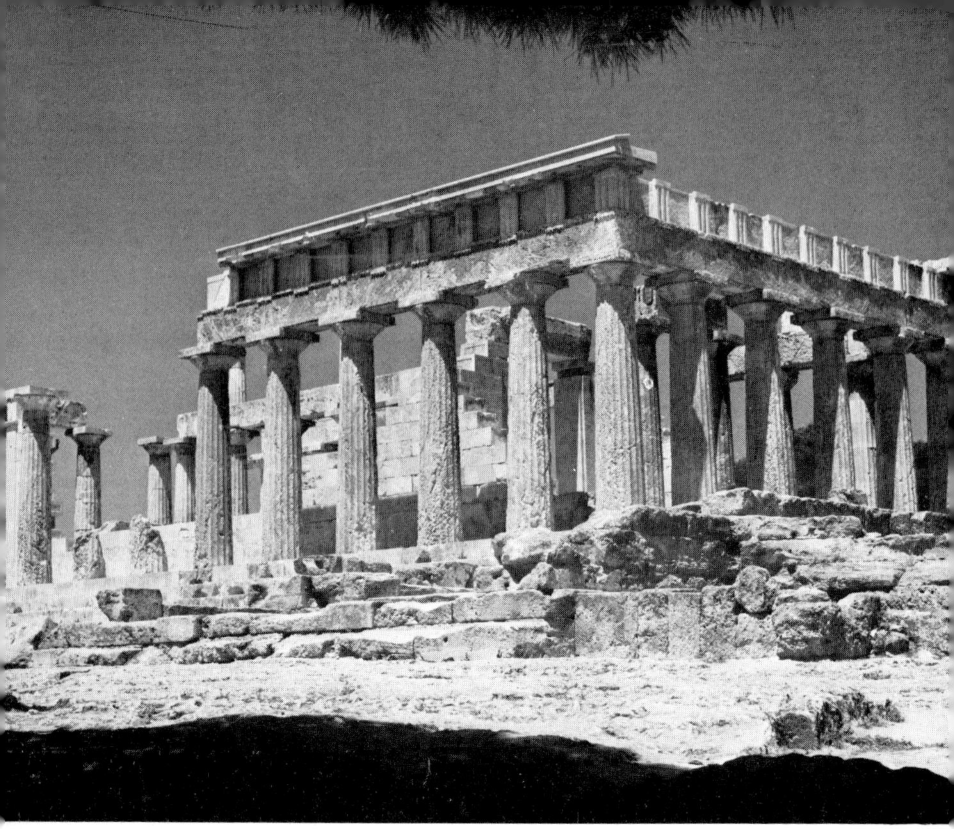

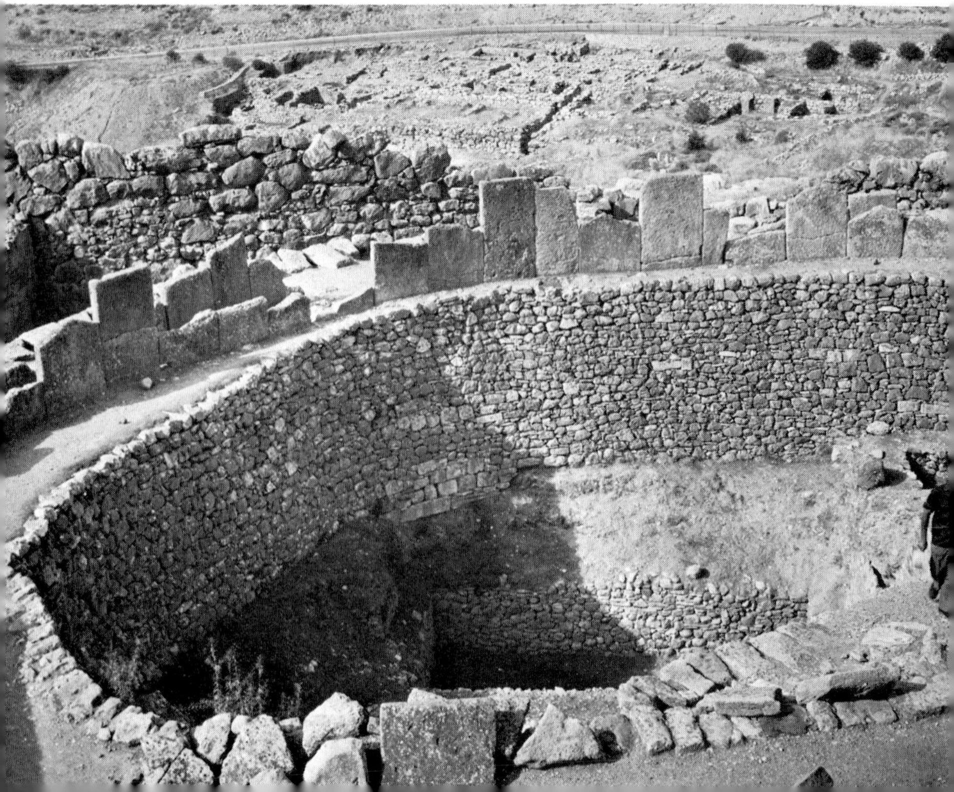

21 *Opposite above* the Temple of Aphea on the island of Aegina;   22   *below* the Royal Tombs at Mycenae

23   Delphi: the Theatre with the Temple of Apollo below

24 Old Corinth

sunglasses worn by almost everyone, winter and summer, are not just against the sun's glare. They disguise what the Spanish are pleased to call 'doslitros' . . . late night circles!

Syntagma or Constitution Square lies on a slight slope. In its central paved area are fountains, orange trees, a public lavatory and a number of pleasantly placed tables over-flowing from adjacent cafes. A lot of local people come here out of season, but when summer tourists take over the regulars seem to migrate to Kolonaki and out-of-town pastures. Three sides of the square are given over to airline offices, travel bureaus, banks, pavement cafes, (where prices are high but the passing show is worth it) and to the façades of the stately Grande Bretagne and King George hotels. The doormen of these two elder statesmen of Athenian accommodation can somehow always get taxis when no one else can. I suspect them of having personal radio connection with the two-way radio taxi systems. For the more humble bus travellers, there are a number of stops on the lower side of the square, useful if wanting to circle Zappeion or making for the Pankrati area, but if you want to enlist the services of the often ancient vehicles, forget all the niceties of queuing. Use elbows, umbrellas and shopping bags like the rest of the would-be passengers. Once wedged inside the door, smiles and an enquiry on where you should alight will bring a dozen answers, a complete conversation on whether you are 'Breetish' . . . there's always some difficulty in distinguishing between American and U.K. citizens . . . and you will find yourself propelled usefully towards your desired destination. It *might* be a stop too early, but you must take the chance! Anyway it is all in the interest of Anglo/Greek relationships.

The fourth side of Syntagma faces the simple, but impressive War Memorial below the Parliament building, where the Evzones, or Presidential Guards, keep constant vigil. In summer, they delight onlookers by their appearance in white fustanellas, long white socks and shoes with huge pompoms, and between their stately patrols, they shelter from the hot sun in little sentry boxes ornamented with striped awnings. The fustanella is a pleated skirt, but don't make the mistake of thinking that this is a feminine garb, any more than the Highland kilt; far from it. The skirt is supposed to have originated with those worn by Roman legionaries and by a band of outlaws known as the Klephts, who made a name for themselves by constantly harrying their Turkish overlords. Nowadays, the fustanella is also adopted as male national dress, as one sees by the multitude of attractive 'dolly' souvenirs, but in practice one sees far more of the baggy trousers and long black boots, though these too are mostly the perogative of the older generations, particularly in the islands. The Guards look rather splendid, for they are all tall young men — I did not realise just how tall until I had the privilege of being invited, one Easter Sunday morning, to partake of the special luncheon given at their barracks behind the Parliament buildings. I was welcomed at the Herodes Atticus entrance by a mountainous sergeant dressed in the dark blue of the winter uniform, and led through to a beautifully decorated courtyard, surrounded on three sides by tall colonnades. Under these, rows of tables were set with bowls of fruit, bottles of wine, and dishes of gaily painted and decorated eggs. On the fourth side of the square was a lower area, and here, there were at least 30 open fires. Over each, a whole lamb was roasting gently upon spits tended by a host of shiningly redfaced and cheerful soldiery, all only too anxious to pose for photographs. Their off-duty comrades strolled importantly in their best blues, towering above their admiring friends and relatives, while waiting for the VIPs to put in an appearance. I felt quite Lilliputian. The lamb was wonderful, succulent and tender, and accompanied by excellent salads, and of course all the other goodies: painted red eggs and limitless bottles of Demestica. There were speeches, cheering, clapping, and dancing and singing by all, regardless of rank or status. It was an Easter celebration not easily forgotten.

Parliament building itself was built originally as a palace for King Otto, designed by Gartner, and partially paid for by Otto's father, the extremely useful Ludwig of Bavaria, in 1843. The Constitution was proclaimed to the new Greek nation from this Palace, and from then, Syntagma Square (Plateia Syntagmatos) received its name. In 1923, after a revolution, refugees from Asia Minor were housed there, and, during the recent military junta, there were no Parliamentary sessions held. Now, it is in full service for both the Chamber of Deputies and for the Council of State. If you are wondering where the royals lived, albeit intermittently, through these years, the new palace is behind the Amalia Gardens in Herodes Atticus. No royal inhabitants now, but Evzones mount guard for the President. You can see them if you walk through the Amalias Gardens, past the ornamental lakes, or past the Exhibition Building in Zappeion Gardens into the street running parallel to Amalias Avenue. You will get better pictures at the War Memorial, as well as the services of the band, when the sentries change guard at 11am, but most people content themselves at the Palace by trying to work out the number of paces in the complicated two step the sentries indulge in. They seem to watch each other most attentively. But possibly that is when one of them is learning the routine.

Through the Gardens again, and across the busy Leoforos Amalias (Amalias Avenue) from Hadrian's Arch is the narrow Odhos Lissikratous, which turns away into the Plaka district, also approached by the twin roads on the lower side of Syntagma Square, called Ermou and Mitreopoulos. I have mixed thoughts about the Plaka. On the one hand I find myself irritated beyond belief by the mass of garish nightclubs, tourist tavernas and souvenir shops which have sprung up like fungi, and, in some cases, disappeared just as quickly. On the other, I never fail to be drawn by the fact that under this veneer of moneymaking a real village, or rather, cluster of villages within a village, still exists without ever lifting its dark head to notice the intruders, however friendly. A little world where the modern age of motorbikes and television masts goes hand in hand with tiny Byzantine churches, Turkish, and even some classical monuments, where a bright patch of flowers, peeping from a tiny garden, distracts one's eye from the incredibly ancient drainage system, but where sunlight endows it all with a faint exoticism. 'Roads' often consist of flights of rather broken-down steps, leading off into slightly unsavoury alleys, and at the highest level, where the roofs make a corrugated salmonpink and brown patchwork quilt over the whole scene, there are the small cottages of the Anafiotika district which clings firmly to the rock of the Acropolis. The people who live here once lived in Anafi, far away in the Aegean Sea, but after Athens was proclaimed capital many workers moved to this ledge and still maintain their own mode of living.

The Plaka seems to indicate 'plaque or flat place', but no part of the Plaka is flat, so wear heels that are firm enough to allow walking where fancy takes you. Descent from the car park under the Acropolis could be by way of the steps beyond the cafe, or you could follow what seems to be the road, and come down by car. I would not really advise the latter unless feeling very daring. We attacked it one day when looking for a short cut, and the upshot was that we drove slap bang into Ifestou, among the souvenir brasses, broken gramophones and mounds of old clothes, and I still do not know how we achieved it. I am also uncertain who was most surprised, but Greek friendliness soon asserted itself and we were guided through with dexterity, cheering and much good-natured banter.

On foot one sees so much more. There are several miniscule Byzantine churches and their size indicates just how unimportant Athens had become in that period. One of these is Sotiraki, or Little Saviour, situated just under the Long Rocks and the caves of the primitives. A short distance away is another, popularly supposed to be associated with Eirene (799/806 A.D.), the empress of Byzantium who was born in Plaka. She was later deified, though I do not understand why, for according to records she murdered her son by blinding him.

Dependent on the flight of steps you have chosen, you will find yourself either beside the Tower of the Winds, or right back on Tripodou, near the junction with Lysicrates Street. Let us take the latter first.

We know that chorus competitions were the original form

of drama which led to Greek drama as we know it. It was the custom of the winners to dedicate their trophies, or *tripos,* to Dionysus, and these were erected either within the theatre precincts or in shrines along the street which led around the foot of the hill to the theatre. During building alterations, seven foundations of such works have been found in the vicinity, and after examination, they were re-buried and left *in situ.* The Monument of Lysicrates had somehow survived, and the inscription within it tells of the people who were to be credited with working towards the prize, much as today we print a list of acknowledgements of help in books, or list credits at the beginning or end of a cinema or television film. Lysicrates' monument was, at one time, part of the library of the French Capuchin convent which stood nearby, and it was known as the Lantern of Demosthenes. Byron, who stayed at the convent, is said to have written part of 'Childe Harold' while sitting within its confines. Later, during the re-occupation of Athens by Omar Vryoni, the convent was accidentally burned down, but thanks to the generosity of the French nation, the monument has been completely restored.

Tripodou turns into Lissiou, and on going ever so slightly downhill, one will see the little Tower of the Winds. Built in the 1st century A.D. as a clock and weather vane, its eight sides, representing the eight winds, have seen their changes too. At one time a Triton figure was the vane, but this disappeared in time. During Turkish rule, the dervishes used the tower as their monastery or *tekke,* and their dancing was a tourist attraction for foreign visitors as well as for local people. Later, before the National Archaelogical Museum was built, it was used as a storehouse for many treasured items. It, like much else in Athens, has undergone a facelift in recent times.

A spot that could also do with such treatment is immediately opposite the tower. Few people notice it, except to remark that it is an eyesore, but it plays a highly important role in history. The derelict doorway has an inscription remarking that it is all that remains of the Mendresse or

Turkish religious seminary. My imagination always takes me irresistibly under the lintel and to the past, for in 1821, when the Turks had learned of the rising tide of revolution, armed members of that community held a meeting at the Mendresse and resolved to kill all Greek males in Attica in an attempt to stamp out any possible rebellion, for, it is reported that they said: 'They are many and we are few.' But the Cadi, Hadji Khalil Effendi, 'a good-hearted man', managed to persuade them to delay such precipitate action for a time, though he agreed to hold leading members of the Greek communities as hostage. His actions saved the lives of at least 4000 men, and might indeed have affected the course of the Revolution itself for a period. One cannot help feeling that the Cadi deserves a tidier memorial than a rubbish heap. . . .

An iron railing surrounds all that is left of Hadrian's Library beside the remnants of what was once the Roman Agora. From the number of times we hear his name mentioned in comparison to other emperors, Hadrian must have acted as a Roman Carnegie to the City of Learning, and it is a pity not to be able to get into this little site, just to get some idea of the extent of another of his gifts. When I mentioned this once, my self-appointed guide airily waved her hand and said 'But that is a modern addition.' Who else but a Greek could think this way!

There are far too many souvenir shops in the Plaka. At the end of the season there are some bargains to be had, particularly if you haggle a little harder than usual. It is usually all very good tempered, and most shopkeepers will go out of their way to please you, so, if one is not quite so helpful, shake off the dust of his or her shop and go find another. I have favourites, to whom I go back year after year, and no doubt when you build up a relationship with Athens you can do the same, but sometimes I find a change of face. Two of us were recently buying the smocky type of shirts which are so useful with jeans, and on finding two we liked, the shopkeeper insisted that we should not buy them without trying them, called for his mother to make room for us in the tiny room at the back of the little store, provided a streaky cracked mirror and left us to our own devices with mother on guard at the door! As they were not exactly gold-plated purchases it would not have mattered . . . but it was the sort of attention that is very much appreciated in this mercenary world.

Across Monastiraki Square from Pandrossou is Ifestou. Whether shopping or just windowgazing and sightseeing, this should not be missed. Go on Sunday morning for fun and crowds, through keep a hand firmly on your wallet or better still leave it locked up at the hotel. On other days you can go to look in leisure and comfort, probably jollied along by the touts en route, though never offensively. One of the things I like best about Athens is that women can walk alone, both by day and in the evening, and very very seldom is there any kind of accosting. As a Greek friend told me during my first visit, 'a girl will be left in peace, unless *she* chooses otherwise'. I think that is still the case, though there may be occasional departures from the norm.

I talked one day with a personable looking youth who spoke excellent English and who had tried to inveigle me into his shop. On finding that I was more interested in writing about Athens than spending money on a lot of rubbish, he was even more entertaining and regaled me with his life history. How much of it was true, I do not know, but it transpired that he had been born into the Pandrossou environment and had always aspired to have a shop of his own, finally making his dream into reality by the age of twenty-four. 'You see', he claimed in the engaging, part boastful, part ingenuous way that Greek youths have, 'I know immediately what someone is looking for, particularly the ladies. Once in my shop, I know I can sell them something'. I felt like singing 'Once aboard the lugger and the girl is mine' . . . but I didn't want to offend him, so I left the would be Onassis to his machinations, and walked further down to call upon Stratos Spiratos. He runs a jeweller's shop at 97 Pandrossou, and, again, we had originally got into conversation because I had gone to ask questions about the district, and had heard him speaking good English to some tourists. On my second visit, he had remembered me even without asking, and despite the hundreds of foreigners who come his way in the course of a year. This time he was again pleased to see me, and even more delighted to tell me that business had been good, and that by summer 1977, he and a friend were opening a small restaurant beside the Russian church along Filenninon. Its name was to be Seven Pans, and I must come and see him there.

'What', I asked, trying to work out how a jeweller could start a restaurant business and hope to succeed, 'do you intend to serve as your speciality'. 'Crepes', he said proudly, 'And Belgian waffles. It will be the first and only place of its kind in Athens. We can't lose' . . . .

I hope he is right. He deserves to succeed, for he works hard. Also he knows the price of freedom. He spent two years in prison in the islands under the junta, because, he once told me, 'I didn't agree with them and said so'. The politics are not important, but the principle is.

Just around the corner from Stratos Spiratos's little shop is the Museum of Greek Folk Art. At least, it used to all be there, but now there are other collections as well, including the one belonging to Paulos Kanellopoulos, housed, at the time of writing, in a renovated mansion on the Plaka side of the Acropolis, and which I have yet to see. There is always something to go back for.

The Museum of Greek Popular Art, Ceramic Collection, is at Areos 1, Monastiraki Square. The building used to be a prison, and before that the mosque of Tsistarakis. Built in 1759, this is the edifice which caused the downfall of the incumbent Governor at that time, because he arranged to use one of the columns of the Temple of Olympian Zeus as part of the building material, and Constantinople was very annoyed by the high-handed action. The small collection is quite well displayed. There are a few items from the last century, but most of the pieces are modern although in traditional forms and designs. This is one of the 'Tuesday closers', so do not try to get in there as a break from shopping on that morning.

Monastiraki Square derives its name from the little church outside which the horsecabs usually take up a stance. The church was originally given the grandiose title Pantanessa or Great Monastery, but locals called it, far more sensibly, little monastery, or Monastiraki, and the name spread to the whole square. All this area was once part of the Turkish Bazaar, and although only the curly-toed shoes, strung like sausages on strings by the shop windows, really remain of the old ways, the atmosphere remains unmistakably Turkish. There are usually nut sellers in the square and their pistachios are usually much cheaper than the ones in the shops, but make sure they are fresh. The vendor will always give you one to try if you are buying. The banner in English across the narrow entrance to Ifestou proclaims Flea Market, so you cannot miss it. The street was named after Haephestus (the erstwhile inhabitant of the nearby Thesion) and much of the trade is still in candlesticks, cauldrons, lamps and scales. Most are made expressly for the tourist trade, probably around the corner or perhaps further along in Astingos. This street bears the name in memory of Frank Hastings, a Phillhellene who fought and died in the Greek War of Independence. It all goes to show just how intertwined classical and modern Athens really are, and the decorative touches of Byzantium complete the intriguing jigsaw of the Plaka district.

These Byzantine churches are not outstanding for their designs when measured against the impressive example, for instance, in Thessaloniki, yet they are worthy of attention. With such a turbulent past it is surprising that they have survived at all. Most of them are within the area of the Plaka, and their miniature scale probably explains why they managed to stay intact while their larger brethren were destroyed. The existing examples are likely to remain with us because it is against the law to pull down churches in Greece. This law has given rise to one rather odd-looking building in Athens. You will see it on your way down Mitreopolis. A tiny church peeps out from a canopy

consisting of a vast modern building built on pillars, so that
the church roof is barely clear of the first floor. It is called
Aghios Dynamis but I have also heard it called Eisodia
Theotokou. It was already occupying the land when the
Ministry of Education elected to build a new administrative
block in the centre of the city. 'All right' said the powers that
be. 'Go ahead, but do not pull the church down'. They didn't,
and you can see the result. On Easter Sunday, and all other
special days in the Greek Orthodox calendar, the congregation flows out beyond the parked cars.

Mitreopolis leads, as its name implies, to the cathedral, a
modern edifice of no particular beauty except that which is
given by the character of the services held there. The large
car park around and in front of it is useful, if you can get
into it on weekdays, but it is the building next door to the
cathedral which is of most interest to visitors from abroad.
Aghios Eleftherios is a gem of Byzantine construction,
mainly because of the interesting collection of materials
used in its building. The foundation of the little cathedral is
attributed to the infamous Eirene, but although the present
building dates, dependent on the source of information,
from eleventh or twelfth century, the stones used certainly
come from some much earlier building of the 6th or 7th
century. These, in their turn date back to the 4th century
B.C.

There is a frieze from this period which represents the
calendar and the months are represented by scenes from the
principal festivals of each month. Cock fighting is there, so
is the grape harvest, there are naked athletes, bull sacrifices,
and so on. When you get as far as the August depiction of the
Panathenaic festival, you will see that a Maltese cross has
been superimposed upon it. Outside, by the south wall,
there is a very ordinary looking block of grey marble. It
bears a Greek inscription claiming that it was used at the
Marriage Feast of Cana in Galilee. Known locally as the
Stone of Cana, it was discovered at Elatea. Look carefully at
some of the mass of indistinct carvings on the walls of the
little cathedral, and you will be able to find the coat of arms

of the La Roche and the Villhardouin families, among the very few reminders of the Crusaders' peaceful sojourn in this part of Greece.

Standing among a host of parked cars mostly belonging to the small boutiques housed in the narrow streets from Ermou, the Kapnikarea is in its own little square and is also attributed to the Empress Eirene. But it is also rather later than her time, so perhaps there was an earlier church on the site. The porch is most attractive, together with a finely decorated marble lintel. Kapnikarea owes its existence to King Ludwig of Bavaria, father of King Otto. It was to have been pulled down in 1834, but he intervened and it was later restored by the University of Athens to its present standard.

The prettiest of the Byzantine churches is not in the Plaka, but hidden away at the back of Klafthmonos Square, off Stadiou. Ayios Theodori was founded in the tenth century but, like the others, underwent alteration and rebuilding in the twelfth century. Unlike the others it has an inscription telling of that work. The belfry was not originally there, but the rest of it is untouched and in the traditional shape, with a little dome.

The flea market is mostly for the tourists nowadays, but the food markets, which run from Monastiraki to Omonia Square are purely Athenian, and they give a very clear picture of the way of life, the manner of purchase, and to the interested cook, some interesting sidelights into the ingredients used in local dishes. The most animated time to visit is on the Saturday morning of Greek Orthodox Easter weekend, which sometimes differs by a week from the Catholic and Protestant celebrations. On this occasion the meat market looks exactly like Christmas in London's Smithfield, but instead of rows of turkeys and geese, the carcasses are serried ranks of lambs of all sizes. Although by our prices they are incredibly cheap, it is often an effort for a family to afford a whole lamb, so that the spending of hard-earned savings is a great occasion, when much prodding, consultation and bargaining is indulged in. Finally, when the drachma have changed hands, father shoulders the meat, and takes it home in a large plastic bag. In the countryside of Attica, the animal ĩs usually purchased on the hoof, but it is carried home across the shoulders in the same fashion.

There is one traditional practice which takes some getting used to—selling trayloads of live day-old chicks in the Athens streets. Each cheeping little fluffy yellow ball is scooped unceremoniously from a tray of his brethren, tipped into a horrid red plastic eggshaped cage and sold to a wide-eyed excited child or his doting parent. Within hours the chick is inevitably dead from cold because it is too fragile to survive alone, and Easter starts with tears. Perhaps that is the idea. The last time I saw this iniquitous practice, an interviewer from Athens radio told me that they have constantly waged war on the air on this unnecessary and cruel habit. Newspapers too have written scathingly, but it continues.

Lambs, eggs, chickens, fruit, flowers, ikons, candles, ribbons . . . all sell at a tremendous pace on Easter Saturday. But there is one item which sells even faster than the rest. Barbecue equipment is necessary for the traditional outdoor roasting ceremony, and the equipment on sale at Easter time is stoutly made, good and cheap. I always look longingly at all the impedimenta cluttering every pavement and every doorway on either side of the market areas, but the airlines might not take kindly to souvlaki sticks, collapsible spits, forks and all the other essentials, so regretfully I have ignored the blandishments of the hawkers.

Long ago, for Greek people as for others, a spring festival celebrated the end of winter, and the return of life to the earth. The ancients worshipped Adonis and Linos, who, legend says, died in early life and were resurrected each spring. In addition there were the stories, already related, of Persephone and Demeter, of the searching across the face of the world for signs of young life, and the division of the year into its seasons. All the festivals took on new meaning with the Christian Resurrection, so that now it is the biggest occasion in the whole Greek calendar, even greater than Christmas, and people travel long distances to be with their families at that time. Good Friday with its pall of sorrow brings long processions from the churches, and if you are in Athens on that morning, you may wish to see the traditional procession from Mitreopolis (cathedral) and which is not unlike others of its kind elsewhere in the Christian world. But the Greek atmosphere does not start to show itself until Easter Saturday night. . . .

It was about 10.30 one Easter Saturday evening when I set off by car to go to Lycabettus Hill. I had debated with myself whether to walk or ride, but concluded that I would get home quicker if I had my own transport. It was not the wisest decision I have ever made. As I drove up the steep roads towards the car park by the open air theatre on Lycabettus Hill I joined a long line of cars, in orderly procession for once, and eventually tucked mine away between two little trees, before joining all the other car owners, now on foot, upwards on the flights of steps towards the little chapel of St George which crowns the summit. If you have ever done this trek you will know that it is quite a long way, but on this occasion I was surprised to see men and women and children, all ages, shapes and sizes, plodding steadily upwards, occasionally pausing for breath in the thin night air, or to admire the lights of Athens winking up all around, before attacking the final steps to the platform around the cafe and the church itself. Despite the numbers on the stairs, I still was not prepared for the vast numbers already in occupation. All Athens, or so it seemed, had come on this night. There was hardly a square yard in which to move about and the parapets were already crammed with people, all of them holding long white unlit candles trimmed with ribbons. It was not an unhappy crowd and was talking, as Athenians inevitably do, but it was a more subdued, far less boisterous gathering than one usually associates with Greece.

I squeezed through the mass of bodies towards the door of the chapel, but it was quite impossible to get within the building. Over the heads of the densely packed, standing congregation, the lights were brilliant and the smell of the great wax candles guttering before the ikons reached me in a warm wave, along with the voices of the clergy. I turned, and struggled back to the area beside the belltower, which also had its fringe of people clinging like living caryatids to their vantage points over our heads. Fortunately I found a small portion of parapet on which I could wedge, but once there it was impossible to move, except outwards into space. It looked an awfully long way down. The hum of conversation grew, small merriments rippled through the waiting crowd, but it *was* still a time of waiting. Then, as my watch hands folded together at midnight, bedlam broke loose. The great bell tolled, deafening us all against the thunder of every other bell in the city, but not against the cacophony of fireworks which also burst against the rock and into our eardrums. The colour of the rockets, the sound of the bells, the burst of song from within the chapel and the sudden brightening and movement of the crowd as friends kissed and embraced each other and everyone around them including me, smiling, singing, crying 'Christos Anesti' (Christ is risen) and then, lighting the long white candles carried so long and so carefully, answering the responses in the service resounding through the loudspeakers, then, slowly, fluidly, overspilling down the steps from the church courtyard, down the sides of the hill in candlelit procession, winking and flickering in the gentle breeze. Far below, and as far as the eye could see, beyond the coloured ring of the rockets, the answering fitful twinkling lights came from thousands of candles flowing like so many glow-worms into the streets of Athens from the doors of all the churches, and one knew indeed that Easter had come to Greece.

Caught up in the emotions, still clinging to my tape-recorder, I, too, started walking . . . caught in the soft illumination from other people's candles, down the long, shallow steps from the mountaintop. People talked still, but quietly, so that the noise from them was more like the steady hum emanating from a beehive than the usual rather shrill tones one associates with Athenian voices. Steadily downwards, round the winding path and past the small tavernas perched on a window sill of a ledge on the side of the Hill.

What a long way we'd come down already, not far now to the foot of the Hill . . . The FOOT OF THE HILL! What was I doing down here? And how could I get back to the car? And, for that matter, where was the car? I stood stock still as the candlebearers flowed riverlike past me, and the horrible truth dawned upon me. Lycabettus Hill is a very large protuberance covering many acres and with a maze of roads, set into one way systems. My car was on the other side of the hill. The only way to get to it from here would be to walk all round the foot of Lycabettus and go up from the other road. Or I could go back up to the summit by the funicular railway. Of course that was it. It was not too late. It would function until everyone was down, surely. There was one slight snag. I hadn't any money, for the few pence I had got for emergency were in the car.

There was nothing else for it. I turned around in my tracks and started upward against the human tide and never have I felt so out of step with my fellow men. But, at the top, at the now almost deserted terrace of St George's it was all worth while. I could just get in to the doorway of the chapel now, to pay my own, rather breathless respects to the Resurrected Saviour before departing down the darkened lonely side of the hill to where a solitary Volkswagen still waited under two guardian trees.

I have said before that Greeks eat late. Easter is one occasion when they eat even later than usual, because most families go home after midnight mass, bringing with them the 'sacred light of the Resurrection' in the form of their candles, and tuck into a meal. This consists of Easter soup, called Maghiriritsa, and of other special dishes. But, before eating, there is yet one more little ceremony. From the bowls placed on tables and around the house, gaily painted and decorated hard boiled eggs are taken, clinked together with another's egg, and the sweet words said again—'Christos Anesti'— Christ is risen.

It is next day, on Easter Sunday that the roasting of the ovelias, as the lambs are called, takes pride of place—after the opening of the gifts of course! Every courtyard, every garden, every balcony, has its charcoal fire and the slowly turning spit where the lamb is basted with a mixture of oil, lemon and oregano, so that the fragrant aroma permeates the whole district. I shall never forget a certain Easter Sunday when I was invited to partake of Easter luncheon with friends in the Kifissia district. Thanks to a change of traffic routes in the back streets of the suburb of which I was blissfully unaware until I got there, I was rather late in arriving, and most of the roasting was completed, but with typical Greek courtesy I was immediately given the opportunity to catch up with wine drinking in the shortest possible time! Consequently it was a distinctly merry party who sat down to the specially prepared Easter bread and cakes, the lamb, the salads, cheeses, yoghourts and fruits, to say nothing of the bowls of hard-boiled eggs in festive reds, yellows and greens.

There was no time to sit and rest after the festive board was cleared. 'Friends are waiting for you and us.' And we all climbed into one car and set off into the Attican landscape. We bumped along a rutted track until we came to an isolated little house surrounded by a large field, where the entire family was assembled to meet us. I was ushered past the roasting spit, into the house and into the main room. This was not a wealthy home but typical of many country homes in the Greek countryside, with one large room with a long table, and small white rooms with little furniture other than beds in them, but the welcome was enormous and universal. Inevitably came the cakes, the bread, the lamb, the wine. . . . I shall never know how I managed to swallow them in order to wish the traditional greetings to my newfound friends, smiling across the oilcloth covered table, toasting each other, in the warmth of comradeship, but with little of each other's language.

Before I left I was presented with a bag containing a little of everything on the table, including several of the red eggs. I was touched by the kindness, but it is only typical of every family that I have every known in Greece.

It might be rather difficult for most tourists in Athens to

see this side of Greek Easter, unless they have friends who invite them to their homes, and yet I am not certain of this. I have been invited by complete strangers to come out to see them . . . even by the custodians at Corinth, who, one would think, would have seen enough foreigners to last them forever. . . . It is not quite so difficult in country areas of course, and in certain towns, such as Lamia, Levadia, Arachova and Amfissa, there are roasteries where traditional Easter meals are cooked for visitors. Of these, I would choose Arachova on the Delphi road, but that is a purely personal choice. Although this village, which clings precariously to the hillside, gets its full share of passing tourists, and there is a clutter of souvenir shops, with some very nice woven goods, most of the inhabitants have not yet been spoiled by the undoubted prosperity that wouldbe consultants of the Oracle have brought them.

4 In revue: Piraeus, the Apollo and Marathon Coasts

I like Piraeus. Melina Mercouri, *Never on Sunday,* and all that. But I did not realise until I happened to be in Piraeus on a Sunday in February, that the film was very well named. *Nothing* happens. At least, if it does, it is very much behind closed doors. Even the ferries, usually the most clamorous inhabitants of Piraeus harbour, doze at their moorings between intermittent trips on winter days, and not even the leanest alleycat scrapes at the dustbins for pickings. Piraeus sleeps.

Piraeus is a rumbustious, riproaring, roystering small city. When a place has been receiving the passing crowd for a couple of thousand years, some of their traits are bound to have rubbed off on the local populace. Apart from Sunday, it is only the siesta hours which bring to the second city that uncanny calm which settles over Greece like a mantle in the afternoon, but in Piraeus one is always aware that it cannot last.

Piraeus was first brought into the role of second leading lady to Athens when Themistocles elected to move the port of Athens from Phaleron further northwards to Piraeus and to base the newly formed Athenian navy there. The move was made because of superior harbouring, but also because there would be more protection for the road to Athens. To assist that process, the Long Walls, stretching all the way from the Hill of the Muses to the port itself, were commenced. It was Pericles who completed the work, and commissioned Hippodamus to plan the new city for Piraeus, and the result was considered to be a model of town planning. It possessed many fine temples and public buildings and we are told that the first trade fairs were held there, a logical choice, in view of the many ships from all nations which moved to and fro in the harbour.

It must have been just as noisy then as it is today. Islanders shove their way on to the waiting ferryboats, taking leave of their relatives and friends in tones that to the uninitiated betoken tremendous quarrels, while ships' sirens shriek warnings of impending departures, nearby factories let forth gasps of protest, and taxis screech round corners on two wheels to deposit their passengers and their baggage unceremoniously at the gangways. They did not have diesel fumes, motorhorns and buses in the 5th century B.C., but no doubt there were equally noxious substitutes.

But perhaps it is at night, most of all, when a burst of laughter carries across the road from a taverna, the thin strains of Greek music echo from a radio in an upstairs flat, a jukebox raucously jangles from a sailors' bar, and men stand anonymously in shadows waiting under the sharp-eyed scrutiny of a 'madam' leaning in a dimly lit doorway, that the real Piraeus shows itself under the neon lights and one realises that nothing has changed one iota.

The northern Long Walls followed roughly the line of the present Odhos Piraeus, which runs between Athens and Piraeus, while the southern Wall ran approximately along the same path as the Elektrikos. There is little trace of either now, for the Long Walls were destroyed by order of the Spartans at the end of the 4th century along with the dockyards. Piraeus, however, continued as a thriving concern, until Sulla ordered its eradication in 87-5 B.C. to prevent it becoming the nucleus of a resistance movement against the Roman Empire. After that time it dropped out of the history books until the advent of the new nation of Greece in the nineteenth century, and it received its present large population in 1922 after the general exodus of Greeks from Asia Minor, when thousands set up what pitiable possessions they had as near as possible to their point of arrival, presumably too weary and too hopeless to go further.

Today, with its industrial smoke, its warehouses and

factories, it is often a disappointing introduction to Athens
for many with only the classical remnants writ large in their
eyes, yet probably it was little different in its disappointment
to those nameless ones for whom it was the entry to the
Promised Land. But in spite of its general lack of beauty, it
has much of interest to the casual observer of everyday
happenings.

If your ship is anchored there for a day or two, it is worth
getting up early to visit the market place off Poseidonos. It
is not far from the new terminal, or from the decrepit one at
Customs House. Just follow the line of the harbour wall until
reaching the Karaiskakis Square, departure point for the
small islands, and plunge into the back streets. The present
market is not quite as colourful as the original one, but is
still fascinating. The fish particularly are always a splendid
sight, for many are unfamiliar to our eyes. Fruit, vegetables,
cheese and sausages, all are different while the barrels of olives
in every hue from palest green to rich plum black gleam
from their oil. Shopping is almost irresistible to the average
woman, until she remembers that she is not going home to
cook! This perhaps is when the advantages of an apartment
or a self-catering holiday become apparent. There are
many shopping streets plunging down to the waterfront in
the main area of the town, and prices are quite good. Choice
of souvenirs along Akti Maouli is probably less than in
Athens, but on the whole so are prices, and a haggle or two
sometimes brings off a bargain.

For the more culturally minded, there is an interesting
little museum on Filellinon, near Passalimani (Zea Marina)
but the magnificent bronzes which were unearthed in July
1959 on the corner of Odhos Filellinon are in the National
Archaelogical Museum in Athens. Make sure you see them
there. There is a magnificent 'kouros', a bronze Athena,
which has been attributed to Kefisodotus, father of the famed
Praxelites, a beautiful bronze Artemis, and a delicate marble
goddess.

The Elektrikos goes directly into Omonia Square from
Platia Karaiskakis and takes about 20 minutes. If you prefer

bus travel, take the No 70 or the 165, which can be found somewhere behind the Tinan Gardens, planted by a French admiral in 1854. You will see an imposing cathedral opposite the gardens. If there are large collections of flowers on the steps it means that a funeral is taking place, and sooner or later, a crowd of sober clothed men will emerge. The original cathedral was destroyed during air raids in 1944, but the plans were still available and after the war it was rebuilt exactly. The Greeks are, despite their volatile exteriors, a most patient people.

From Piraeus, a corniche of sorts rounds the coast towards several smaller harbours. Along it is the naval academy and an ancient tomb which legend maintains is that of Themistocles, and all that is left of the Walls of Konon. The first harbour reached is Zea Marina, still often referred to as Passalimani (harbour of the Pasha). During excavations in the nineteenth century, the outlines of the former sheds in which ships were housed were found here, for this was once the ancient port of Zea. If you visit the Naval Museum in the vicinity, you can see a model of how it must have been, together with models showing the battles of Salamis, the Wars of Independence and of the Second World War. Today, Zea has a more peaceful occupation. It is the most important marina in Greece, and apart from being the departure point for the one-day cruises to the islands, offers shelter to thousands of small, and not so small, privately owned craft from every nation. The promenade is pleasant, with several nice little cafes and restaurants, as well as a full cargo of ship's chandlers whose windows provide numbers of unknown items for landlubbers, and splendid purchases for the more knowledgeable seagoing fraternity.

Kastella, once Munychia, has a lovely view from the top of the hill, taking in as it does the three beautiful harbours and the wide expanse of the Saronic Gulf. The descent into Microlimano is very steep, but it is comforting to know in this land of erratic drivers there is a one-way system for cars, so there is a little less danger than one imagines at first sight. Microlimano means 'little harbour', but again, it is still often called by its old name of Tourcolimano, or Turkish harbour. Pretty enough in daytime with its white houses and perfectly curved bay, it comes into its own at night as a favourite place for evening excursions to the fish restaurants lining the harbour wall. Take your time choosing among them despite invitations from the waiters touting for business. Further details will be found in the chapter dealing with Tips for Tourists. Long before the advent of the Turks, Microlimano had another name, for in ancient times it was the port of Munychia, and under the water on the northern side of the harbour, where the present slipways are, can be seen the remains of the ones once used by the triremes. A No 2 bus comes to Microlimano and to Passalimani from the Electric Railway Station at Piraeus.

Once out of Microlimano and pointed along the coastal road there is little to see. At the moment of writing the whole area is undergoing reclamation and general redevelopment and if the problem of pollution can also be solved this would become a most attractive area, particularly in view of its proximity to Athens. Certainly almost anything would be an improvement on its present condition, but we should not pass it without a glance. Here was the original port for Athens, and it was from here that Theseus departed to fight the Minotaur in the labyrinths of Knossos on Crete. More certainly, it was also here that the flying boats used to pause for rest on their passage to India and Australia in the 1920's, when Imperial Airways blazed their route Eastward. No trace of any of it now, but just knowing where it all happened helps to clothe the skeletons of history in living flesh.

Past the airport at Ellenikon (where the terminal buildings were built to one of the last designs executed by the famous Finnish architect Eero Saarinen), until we reach Glyfada. It is a nice little resort, particularly popular with Athenians, who flock there in summer. They do not seem to be bothered by the constant aircraft but they are probably too busy taking their pleasures equally noisily. You can always tell the difference between locals and foreigners even without looking at hair colourings. All the foreigners are intent on soaking up the sun, and lie supine on the beaches as motionless as ancient statuary. The Greeks are always talking and 'busy' though at what is not always obvious.

Many holidaymakers prefer to go further down the coast, and Voula and Kavouri have become favourite spots, with tavernas, a pleasant atmosphere and a beach (small fee required). Still further along, Vouliagmeni has become very popular too, mainly because of its public beach, a delightful little marina with luxury facilities for over 100 yachts and a pleasing restaurant with lovely views, all run by the National Tourist Organisation of Greece. The small peninsula is topped by the Astir Palace which must qualify as one of the most exclusive hotels in Greece, and which has its own beach, sports facilities, restaurants etc, but there are also a number of smaller premises, pensions, flats etc in the close vicinity. Although it is quite a long way into central Athens, many visitors prefer to stay in this area, so that they may get the best of both worlds, particularly in summer. The original popularity of Vouliagmeni came from the reputed healing properties of its lake and the sulphur region, but now it has a much wider appeal and justifiably so. Further down the coast, too, is another attractive holiday spot, at Lagonissi, but it is, I think, just too far to be useful for Athens sightseeing. Better to go there and laze when the footslogging is finished.

Like most visitors it is the sea which attracts me back to this lovely coastal road and the endless vistas of sea and sky which come at every turn. But it is being eroded gradually and not by the elements. Each time I visit, I see an increasing number of houses, villas and holiday complexes springing up.

The Apollo Coast terminates at one of the most famous and exquisite places in Greece, and every visitor should make the pilgrimage to Poseidon's temple at Sounion at least once in his life. Most arrive there during the day, when the light is blinding, the heat bounces from the rocks, the strings of coaches are jockeying for position, and the little tourist pavilion is overloaded with hungry and thirsty customers, yet it is still impressive. But if you possibly can, go out of season, preferably in winter, and as near sunset as you can, even if you have to drive back to Athens in the dark. The setting is tremendous. Set high on a promontory, the temple is about ten years older than the Parthenon, and it is thought to have been designed by the same architect responsible for the Thesion. It was not the first temple to be built on this site for there had been an earlier edifice, also dedicated to Poseidon. This had been made of porous stone and was badly damaged during the Persian Wars. Some of the original materials were incorporated into the later building, in which there were 34 Doric columns of which only 15 remain standing, but they are without doubt some of the most photogenic ruins in the world. Byron loved Sounion and wrote in 'Don Juan': 'Place me on Sounion's marble steep . . . there swanlike, let me sing and die'.

He sang loudly enough in one way, disfiguring one of the columns by scrawling his name upon the lovely grey-veined white marble. Incidentally, most Doric columns have 20 grooves, but the Sounion ones have only 16. It is thought that the marble must have been brought from the Agrileza quarries four kilometres away, which must have been in use at that time. There is a Paros marble frieze, showing battles between Centaurs and Lapiths, together with the exploits of Theseus. It is protected by a wooden shelter to the east of the pathway up the incline, but once it must have looked down upon the regattas which were held in Sounion Bay below the Sacred Cape, in honour of the mighty God of the Sea. You can also see, on a lower hill, some other ruins of a temple. These were once dedicated to Athena of Sounion. There really are some remarkable instances of 'hedged bets' in ancient Athenian history!

Ten miles north east of Sounion along the coastline is Lavrion, once the site of the silver mines of ancient Athens, and whose wealth enabled Themistocles to build the Athenian naval strength to the point where it could survive the Persian onslaught. Today one goes to Lavrion to catch a ferry to the island of Kea. Further along is Thorikos, another city-state in Attica of which only a small portion remains, including the theatre. There is an echo of King Minos here, for the legends tell that the consort of the king of Thorikos ran away to Crete to live joyously with the Cretan king. From Thorikos, the countryside of the Messogia is thankfully still typical and unspoiled and there are many vineyards in this region as well as many opportunities to sample the products in roadside tavernas around Koropion and Peania, though the roads are winding enough without adding alcoholic embellishment!

Many Athenians have holiday homes along the coast, but it has never become a foreign tourist venue, possibly because there is little land available for hotel complexes near the sea, for many large houses also have long stretches of coastline within their grounds and it is almost impossible to get to the beach in some areas. Pine trees afford welcome shade along the accessible beaches, much favoured by the camping fraternity in summer. One winds in and out to the coast along narrow lanes, as there is no main coastal road, and alleged 'short cuts' take one bumping along rutted farm tracks suitable only for four wheel drive vehicles and the goats one encounters.

Porto Rafti is pretty, with a small island keeping guard over the entrance to the land-locked bay. On the island is a Roman statue representing what is thought to be a tailor. Hence the name 'Port of the Tailor'. Further along, Vravrona has a good little museum, showing some of the finds at the site of the partially reconstructed temple of Artemis. In ancient times, the goddess was considered to be the patron of fertility and birth, and the Athenian women came in procession every four years to this temple. One would have to have been enthusiastic or desperate for it is a long walk from Athens. Now you can get there by car, or by one of the local bus services from Macromateon Street.

It is not far, either, if you are in private transport, to Rafina, a sleepy little town whose main claim to fame is that is the departure point for Evia and the Cyclades, and I never watch the passengers embarking without a sense of desolation at being left behind. The fish auctions on the slope down to the ferry are always interesting for their mounds of squid and octopus, and often good small shellfish, and the tavernas here supply excellent cooked versions of whatever is on sale, at a reasonable price. At the top of the hill, Plaka cafe has beer, coffee, cakes and Metaxa at fair prices, and many are the occasions I have sought refuge there from the winter winds which bite hard on this coast. But, thank heaven, the winter is short, and one soon reverts to the chairs and tables at the door and the blessed spring sun, which warms the blood and the bones of Attica. Around and beyond Rafina, there are many pleasant little beaches, which are now getting their share of holiday visitors from overseas, for there are unsophisticated hotels and restaurants and a camping site at Nea Makri, but, if you are to complete your pictures of Athenian classical history, you must go a little further still, to Marathon.

Marathon. The word has come into our language and stands for endurance, a long test, or the long running of anything from a film to a horse race, but it comes to us from courage, and from a battle which took place in the swampy ground of the bay of Marathon, between the sea and the mountains and somewhere about four kilometres from the modern village of the same name. The Athenians, assisted by the Plateians, who were doughty fighters, and led by General Militiates, met the Persian forces on 16 August 59 B.C., and, outnumbered as they undoubtedly were, succeeded in forcing the opposition to fight in the marshes, where the heavy armour of the Persians proved their undoing. When victory was assured, a runner was sent racing across the lower hills of the Pentelikon range to bring the glorious news to Athens. He ran without pause, forcing himself onwards at a cruel rate, and as he reached the Acropolis and gasped out his tidings, he died from exhaustion. Just outside the village of Marathon, which incidentally has several tavernas and a tiny 'supermarket', there is a marble platform, surrounded by a march of flagpoles. This is the starting place for the Marathon races held today.

At the site of the actual battle, there is also a marble. It is a white relief copy of the Warrior of Marathon and it stands beside a mount called the Soros. It is the reputed burial place of 190 Athenians who fell in the battle, and excavations have confirmed that ashes and calcined bones together with small possessions from the 5th century B.C. are indeed contained within it. There are many local stories of the ghosts of Marathon, and while, in summer, when the cafes, car parks and even the steps leading to the top of the Soros are sprinkled with tourists of every nation, one can smile tolerably and dismiss the tales as peasant superstition, twilight on an autumn evening, when the laughing voices of the tourists are stilled and only the winds whistle across the marshes produces a very different atmosphere.

There were two lively dogs who had no such inhibitions when I went to Vrana. I had been to the recently excavated Tomb of the Plateians, a mound of stones containing the skeletons of many young men. I had wanted to see the place where the warriors depicted on the frieze on the Temple of Athena Nike were buried. Then, I made my way across a field at the far end of Vrana to try and find the Helladic grave circles I knew to be there. The dogs galloped out of a small cottage to meet me, falling over each other in their enthusiasm to meet the mad foreigner, and they made such a racket that they roused their owner, a little woman, whose dark eyes glowed at me across the top of a scarf wound tightly across her nose and mouth, a common practice in this part of Attica at all seasons other than high summer. They also brought the caretaker out of the nearby research building. He very kindly forsook his lunch to produce the keys and show me round. The graves are indeed circles, protected under a large temporary shelter, and the skeletons, from the middle or late Helladic period, are still in their burial places. There is also an extraordinary skeleton of a Prze-walski type horse, which was found as recently as 1970. It is not until one sees these little excavations in the middle of nowhere that one realises that all over the world, and not only in Greece, people devote their lives to resurrecting the past, not for themselves nor for their own glory, but for their children's children.

If you have time, before turning reluctantly citywards again, you could go on to Ramnous to see the remains of the two temples. The smaller dates from the 6th century B.C. and was dedicated to Themis, Goddess of Justice, but was destroyed by the Persians. After the victory at Marathon, the second temple was erected. It was to Nemesis, Goddess of Vengeance and indeed there is a certain brooding atmosphere here. Perhaps the goddesses are a little annoyed that humanity has so easily forgotten their existence.

The road back to Athens from the east coast goes through Kifissia, that pleasant shaded little resort which is now considered a better-class Athenian suburb. In classical times, out-of-town dwellers were called *peroikoi,* or 'round about', because they were shut off from the democratic privileges of the city and unprotected from attack. It must have improved in Roman times, because Herodes Atticus, that indefatigable builder of memorial theatres and stadiums, had a villa in Kifissia. The site is now covered by the Cathedral of St Demetrius. Today when the Elektrikos reaches right to Omonia from Kifissia, the Kifissians certainly have a pleasant place in which to live, yet can reach Athens very quickly indeed. There are a number of small hotels in the area, and some excellent restaurants and tavernas used by many local people. I suggest that when the heat in Athens gets too great you follow their example and spend the evening in shady Kifissia.

Another evening sortie could be to Mount Parnes, reached by teleferique or a sinuous mountain road and where there is a nightclub and casino, but 'Never on Tuesdays'. An afternoon excursion might be to the monastery at Kaisariani. There is a spring on the hillside below the monastery, which, at one time, was said to have magical powers in curing infertility. I have no wish to cast aspersions on the beliefs of others, particularly on those of former generations, but I seem to remember that monasteries in Britain some centuries ago had springs near them, which were credited with equally magic powers.

It all goes to show that excursions from Athens could possibly have some remarkable effects on occasion!

5 Greek drama:
more excursions from Athens

'After these things, Paul departed from Athens and came to Corinth.' It was on a gold-washed spring morning that, once again, I found myself following the example of the Apostle who, over the years of wandering in Mediterranean countries, I have come to regard as the First Tourist, for wherever I go, his name crops up again and again, and I find myself wondering what his reaction was. This time, I took the old road, as he must have done, which is now called Iera Odhos, past Plato's Academy, through the working suburbs where the haphazard shops were opening in their usual lethargic manner. Rain had fallen heavily in the night, and the rugged road surface had great puddles through which traffic and pedestrians alike splashed unheedingly, so that, within a short time, my reasonably clean windshield had a fine layer comprising old motor oil and mud. By the time I reached Dafni, where the old road joins the motorway, I could hardly see through it in safety, so I got out to clean it. As I did so, I looked across the road to where the iron gate into the grounds of Dafni Monastery stood half open. It is a sad fact of a journalist's life that there never seems to be time for everything to be done at leisure but I'd long promised myself to take a quick look round at Dafni. I looked at my watch. There was just time before pressing on for an appointment at Corinth. I tucked the car off the road and walked into the grounds and into the shade of the tall cypresses.

The name Dafni means laurel, and in ancient times this plant was connected with the worship of Apollo. It seemed right that I should be visiting Dafni on such a sunny morning for there was a temple to the Sun God on this spot long before Christianity came to Greece, so St Paul must have come right past that temple on his journey to the Roman capital at Corinth. The temple was destroyed in the 4th century A.D. and, when the monastery was built in the 5th century, it was from the materials still available on the site. The monastery was dedicated to the Virgin and remained so for centuries. In 1205, it was handed over by Othon de la Roche, the recently appointed Duke of Athens, to the Cistercian monks from Bellvaux in Burgundy. At that time it was considered to be among the finest monasteries in the area, with exceptionally splendid mosaics, of which there are some remnants. In time, the monastery was again appropriated, this time by the Greek Orthodox monks, so that there are small remnants from various ages in this miniature citadel of religious history. There are two sarcophagi in the courtyard, both ornamented with fleurs de lis. We are told that they belong to Othon de la Roche and to Gauthier de Brienne, but Demetrios Sicilianos says in his fascinating book, *Old and New Athens,* that it is Guy II, the last de la Roche, who is buried there and that Othon returned in 1225 to his native land, together with his wife and two sons and died there nine years later. You may take your choice. In any case it is the mosaics that one comes to see.

I must admit that at first, I was sorely disappointed, but, like so much else in Greece, it takes time to discover their beauty. 'The entry into Jerusalem' is a case in point, for in this it is the method of drawing the perspective of the feet which is the most unusual feature for a mosaic of this era. But it is the portrait of Christ above one's head in the cupola which has the most lasting effect.

The road which climbs over the brow of the hill above Eleusis town is an extremely busy one. It has always been so, mostly with travellers going in the other direction, but of course the present road is comparatively new. It was little more than a track for years, and John Hobhouse, coming from Thebes in 1809 with Byron, must have come somewhere near this way, and must have been thankful to get there for he wrote 'on arriving at Athens you there perceive an

agreeable change in the aspect of all around you'. Three
years before, Chateaubriand, that elegant adventurer whose
name we associate with a succulent steak, stayed in the
unsalubrious, probably flearidden, little town of Eleusis
before making his ceremonial arrival at Athens; but not all
visitors were so peacefully inclined. Fourteen hundred years
before him, the Goths, under Alaric, crossed the pass of
Dafni, to be halted, we are told, by 'a vision of Achilles and
Athena' and, still further back in the mists of time, the
ancients travelled these last miles on the long trek from
Delphi, and inevitably, paused to pay homage at the great
shrine which then stood at Eleusis.

The 'owners' of that shrine, Demeter and Persephone,
would hardly approve of the town of Eleusis today, as far as
its contributions to the environment are concerned. It covers
the surrounding countryside with a libation of white cement
dust, lights the gathering dusk with flames from its ship-
building furnaces, and refines the sacred olive oil for
commonplace domestic use. But it was once among the foremost religious centres, rivalling Delphi and Delos in importance. Eleusinian rites have retained their mysteries
throughout the centuries. The initiated dared not reveal their
content and the uninitiated could only guess vaguely at the
secrets but as it is reported that the ceremonies were accompanied by suggestive dances, obscene songs and gestures,
performed in torchlight processions, it is likely that the
whole would have qualified for an 'X' certificate in today's
ratings, even in our permissive society.

The Eleusis archaelogical site is obviously, therefore, one
of great importance, but it is very difficult to maintain a
romantic image when one has to plough through factories to
reach it, and in consequence it has become one of the least
popular for the average tourist. However, it is rich archaeo-
logically and excavations have shown that the area has been
inhabited since pre-history by a succession of peoples,
including Myceneans. The museum has an excellent selection
of findings, including a huge amphora from the 7th century B.C. which has interesting decorative motifs showing

the blinding of Polyphemus by Odysseus, Perseus killing the Medusa etc. So these legends *were* legends even then. One feels newborn in the presence of such antiquity. They will last longer than we.

The new road to Corinth along the hillside runs parallel with legend as well as with history. The history lies in the offshore island of Salamis, scene of the great battle with the Persians. The legend is in the Scironian rocks, where the notorious Sciron stopped peaceful travellers, compelled them to wash his feet while standing on the edge of the precipice, and then kicked his luckless victims into the sea where a giant turtle had them for breakfast. Theseus dealt with Sciron eventually by throwing him over the cliff as turtlebait, and it is while pondering the risks of journeying this coast as it was, and comparing it with the risks engendered by the stupidity of drivers today, that one arrives at the canal almost without realising it.

The first time I saw the Corinth Canal was at night from the deck of a small ship. The towering walls of concrete on either side of the vessel, the floodlights illuminating our passage, the general feeling of enclosure, imprinted itself on my memory forever. I feel that there is no other way to see the Canal apart from this. From the narrow spans of the road and foot bridges the chasm is deceptively mild, and it isn't until one takes a series of pictures with a zoom lens that the magnitude of the achievement is realised.

The Corinth Canal is relatively modern. It was opened on 6 August 1893 by King George the First of the Hellenes, but it had long been considered as a possibility. In ancient times ships were drawn across the top of the Isthmus to avoid the long sea journey. It was thought that if cuts were made deeply into Mother Earth to facilitate the passage of the ships, the earth would bleed, and it would incur the wrath of the gods. In 600 B.C., Periander put forward a plan for the development but it was dropped some 300 years later, mainly because it was thought that the sea level in the Corinthian Gulf was higher than the Saronic Gulf and would flood the land. Julius Caesar and then Caligula played with the idea, but it was Nero who began the work. He opened the workings by using a golden shovel and carrying the soil away in a basket. Then he gave the project over to the ministrations of some 6000 prisoners of war. It has always been claimed that they were mostly Jewish. The scheme was abandoned when the clouds of rebellion in the Western Provinces of Gaul and in Spain and Africa began to gather over the Roman Empire and Nero returned to his capital, and to eventual suicide. It was not until after the liberation of Greece that the plan was seriously considered again, but the Greek nation did not have the money at that time. A French company started work in 1882, went bankrupt in 1889 and left the work to be completed by a Greek company in 1893. Perhaps in all this is some consolation for the promoters of the Channel Tunnel.

There are a few shops and souvlaki sellers on the Peloponnese side of the Canal and there is plenty of parking space. I bought a little corn dolly there one day, which now hangs above my kitchen window. Whenever I feel a little low, I turn it around and it seems to bring a new burst of luck. Maybe Demeter has some hand in the proceedings; after all, Corinth is not so far from her headquarters at Eleusis.

The present town of Corinth is a rather boring, flat place, but it is not entirely its own fault. The area has long been subject to earthquakes, and a constant succession of towns has been destroyed by them on this site over the centuries. The last tremors were in 1928 and since then the township has been rebuilt in antiseismic style. The main products of the area are raisins and currants and at harvest time, trays of them can be seen laying in the sun to dry, but you will miss little else by avoiding the town completely and making straight for old Corinth by driving on the road through the fragrant vineyards and orange groves towards the mountain crowned by the citadel of Acro-Corinth. The present village is built on the site of ancient Corinth near old Lachaeum, and the archaeological site is part of it as it almost cowers from the wind off the sea. Certainly one gets the impression that the present small population is purely a continuance of the long line of inhabitants, for standing in the ruins, near the wall, far from the little obedient clumps of guided tours, one suddenly hears the clang of goatbells and sees, just along the adjacent road, a solitary small figure, guiding home a miniature flock. Then, just as the figures change along an ancient frieze, a horse clip clops along the same roadside, and a bell tolls. Corinth lives still.

According to myth, the town was founded by Sysyphus, grandfather of Bellopheron, owner of the great winged horse Pegasus, and this is why so many representations of them can be found on Corinthian vases and mosaics. Before Athens came to supremacy, Corinth enjoyed a period of great wealth, but it was not until the decline of Athens that Corinth became the seat of the Achaean League. The Romans destroyed the city completely in 146 B.C. and for a whole century no one dared to raise it, but Julius Caesar rebuilt it in 44 B.C. and set up a colony called Laus Julia Cronthiensis. It was a cosmopolitan community composed of people from many races and creeds, Greeks, Orientals, Romans, Syrians, and Jews, but the main religions were still those of the ancient gods. The main temple whose ruins we can see today was still dedicated to Apollo and there were others to Athena, Poseidon, Hermes, to Venus and many more, and, playing safe, no doubt, a temple dedicated to 'All the Gods', named the Pantheon. But the ones which attracted most worshippers were those dedicated to Asklepios and his daughter Hygeia, the god and goddess of healing, and perhaps most attractive of all, the temple of Aphrodite, situated high on the mountain peak of Acro-Corinth.

According to Strabo of Amasia, writing in the 1st century B.C. 'The sanctuary of Aphrodite is so wealthy that it possesses as slaves of the temple more than 1,000 courtesans who were dedicated to the goddess both by men and women, and so, by reason of them, the city was thronged and enriched, for the sailors spent their money easily and, on that account the proverb says "Not for every man is the voyage to Corinth".' No wonder that by the time St Paul arrived in

51-2 A.D., it was a wealthy, expensive and already degenerate city, and that the unbending Apostle found it necessary to address such reproaches to its inhabitants.

The area excavated is only a small portion of the ancient city which, surrounded as it was by a wall stretching to the port of Lachaeum, covered a vast area. But it is a most telling section. Streets, squares, baths, porticoed shopping precincts, temples, even a public latrine with seats above a water-flushed drain. Apropos of this last 'mod con', I am reminded that for centuries urine was an essential ingredient in the making of coinage. The Roman Emperor Vespasian taxed the purchase of collections from public lavatories, and when his son Titus reproached him for it the Emperor is said to have produced a coin and asked 'Does this stink?', hence the phrase 'filthy lucre'.

The Bema, where St Paul is reputed to have defended the Christian faith is marked clearly. We know that the Jewish community of Paul's time is very likely to have come to Corinth after expulsion from Rome by Claudius. The dates coincide with those of the arrival of Aquila and Priscilla whom Paul met in Corinth, but we do not know where the synagogue was situated, although an interesting inscription was found on a large stone, probably from the lintel of a doorway, at the foot of the steps leading to the agora from the Lachaeum Road. It proclaims simply 'Synagogue of the Jews' and dates from about the 5th century A.D. It is likely that the site of the synagogue would have remained the same even if the building was renewed over the years. The section of the road which is excavated is almost perfect, and this must be due to the fact that no wheeled traffic could negotiate the stepped surfaces. When H. V. Morton wrote his splendid book about the Great Apostle, he must have felt that here indeed, he walked 'In the steps of St Paul'.

One of the most interesting remains is that of the fountain of Peirene, mentioned by that other fountain of knowledge, Pausanias. The fountains are supposed in legend to have sprung from the tears of Peirene for the death of her son. The fountain house has several arches, behind which is the reservoir, and you can if you wish climb inside, but it is rather slippery and none too clean, and it is all to easy to crack one's head. Nowadays, the water is carried away by pipes to the 'modern' village outside the excavations, so that the whole effect is rather spoiled.

There is also a sacred spring which dates from the 6th century B.C. It was for some reason sealed and hidden during Roman times, for they were ignorant of its existence. It still possesses two rather nice lion heads from which the water must have flown. I always enjoy hours spent at ancient Corinth, scrambling over masonry, walking the tiny cobbled streets where in spring there is a riotous display of flowers.

Armed with a satisfactory map, Corinth is one of the most exciting places to visit, for it always surprises with something new that one has not noticed before. The museum too has a lot of interesting exhibits, and those gathered from the Asklepion always evoke a great deal of comment. It was the custom, and still is in the Greek Orthodox Church, to place models of the afflicted part of a body and which the supplicant wished to be healed, in the Temple. Remembering the nature of the Temple of Aphrodite on Acro-Corinth, and supposing that the models were accurate representations of the worshipper's anatomy, there were some very strange sights and shapes to be found in ancient Corinth.

All the time I was in the area of the city on my first visit, I was conscious that something else was pulling at my coat-tails to move on. 'Come', it whispered, 'Come up here'. And so it was that I climbed back into the car, and started on the long steep lane, past the little cottages and the fields, upwards towards the first old gateway that marks the entrance to the fortressed Acro-Corinth peak. It is quite a long, winding climb for a car, let alone if on foot, but finally one comes to a small area beside a hopeful little cafe where the car can be left safely, and from then on, one is on one's own. The fortified wall runs up hill and down dale, following the contours of the mountainside in a great encircling movement and the main cobbled road to the second and third gateways climbs even more steeply from the first sturdy entrance. The whole area was aflame with poppies, not the light red variety associated with Flanders, but dark rich blood red with spiky black centres. There was not a soul in sight, except for a couple of distant goats, but the atmosphere was immediate. It was friendly, flower scented in the sunlight, alive with the humming of insects as bees rushed hither and thither and unseen crickets sang. It said at once that many people had lived on this mountainside. I walked onward, upward, back into time, while the landscape of Greece widened below me and melted into the sunlit distance.

From Mycenean times, Acro-Corinth has known humanity. In that period it had a small citadel and it was always to be the scene of many bloody conflicts. Plutarch claimed that in the early days it was so strong a fortress that 100 men and 50 dogs could garrison it. The Macedonians knew that if they wanted to dominate the area they had to hold Acro-Corinth, known as one of the two horns of the Bull of the Peloponnese (the other was Ithome in Messenia), and the political and commercial power of Corinth depended to a great extent on the fortifications of the citadel on the mountaintop. For a military minded man, Acro-Corinth is fascinating. So many armies have contributed to its fortifications and dwelt securely within its fastnesses, Byzantines, Crusaders, Venetians, Turks, and each addition has been in a different architecture. One stumbles over great stones, wells, ancient cannon mountings, old buildings which once must have held the quartermaster's most precious stores, but still one goes upward, inevitably drawn by the summit, despite the gathering clouds and the slowly rising wind. At the very pinnacles, for there are, surprisingly, several ragged outcrops around the fortress stones, the view is of all Greece. Lesser hills hump sulkily below a patchwork green blanket and on a fine day, one can see both the Saronic and the Corinthian gulfs, surmounted by a backdrop composed of the Peloponnese mountains. Rough, gnarled, eroded foundations are all that is left of the basilica which replaced Aphrodite's temple, though the stones, both of the basilica and the temple, were used later by the Turks for the construction of a mosque.

I am never quite sure how the excursion buses manage to fit in Corinth, Epidaurus, Nauplion and Mycenae in one day, but they do. It is a masterpiece of organisation, and for those with little time at their disposal, an excellent way of seeing some of the most important sites in Greece. Guides are usually very knowledgeable, and have a knack of covering most of the salient points, but with few exceptions they are inevitably in a hurry, sounding their rallying cry and rounding up their stragglers like sheepdogs.

The best guide I ever had was not of this ilk. I was on a visit to Delphi, long ago. He was an old man, and frail, but he knew every stone and every corner of the navel of the earth as if it was part of his own body. At one point, he sat, my modern Socrates, on a rock under the shade of an olive tree while we, his disciples, grouped around him, sandwiches unheeded, while he painted a picture of ancient Greece that I have never heard bettered.

'And here' says the guide, as we plough up the dusty path behind groups of tourists chattering in every tongue, 'we are coming to the famous Lion Gate'. Cameras click obediently, but some of us wait until the crowd clears sufficiently to allow us to climb on fallen masonry in the hope of getting a better view. It isn't. The light isn't falling on the lion's heads. Next time perhaps. There just has to be a next time for these sites, and as a friend of mine is very fond of remarking 'Nothing good can be done in five minutes'.

The approach to Mycenae is not at all as one expects it to be. The ruins are camouflaged into the hillside so that it is not until one is almost upon them that they begin to take shape, into an Acropolis where the Palace of Agamemnon once commanded a view of the Argive plain. This was a very necessary precaution in the centuries between 1600 and 1100 B.C., for these communities were in a constant state of war with each other and the citadels, built on certain strategic hills, could embrace the unprotected people working on the lands below within their walls until the dangers had passed once more. In the Argolid, certainly Mycenae and Tiryns secured the safety of the Myceneans, just as the Acropolis at Athens looked after the area of Attica. The myths and legends which surrounded all these states were handed down and it was due to Heinrich Schliemann's implicit belief that Homer had recorded them accurately and that they were based in truth, that led to his eventual discovery of the great gold treasures of the royal burials at Mycenae. One is almost impatient of the long prologue spoken by the guides when they pause outside the Lion Gate to explain about the building of the citadels. It is the burial places that are the stars in this show, not the safety curtains. Nevertheless, the lions must have their share of the limelight for they are the hallmark of Mycenae, and at last the moment comes when one stands on the narrow walks which surround the royal cemetery inside the Acropolis.

Grave Circle A, excavated by Schliemann in 1876, lies to the south side of the Lion Gate and consists of a circular enclosure with rows of slabs set vertically. The space between the two rows was filled with small stones and roofed by more slabs, so that there was a small circular wall. Inside the graves in the western area were six family tombs. They varied in size according to the number of people they contained but undoubtedly the bodies were those of people of high birth by reason of the wealth which was interred with them. Men, women and children were found there, together with many of the richest and most important items now in the National Museum, and it is no wonder that Schliemann was convinced that he had found Agamemnon himself. I must say that I like to cling to his beliefs, despite all the later forensic evidence to the contrary. It makes it all just that bit more exciting somehow. I am not sure what other people expect at these circles. For me, after the intense interest engendered by seeing the treasures in the Museum, the thrill of simply arriving at Mycenae and actually seeing the Lion Gate it was almost an anticlimax to stand at the grave circles. There were too many schoolparties, too many holidaymakers, too many irreverently curious feet and eyes peering into the blank graves so that all the atmosphere departed. But on other, less hectic visits, when arriving without the hordes, one can stand silently in the wind which sometimes blows across these inhospitable hills and the circles make a much bigger impact.

It is worthwhile, if you have the time, going to the Palace at the top of the hill, despite the steep incline. Whether the graves were of Agamemnon and his family or not, this is the view that he had over his city, and the outline of the palace, where he lived and to which he returned only to be murdered, is here for us to see. Electra, Clytemnestra, all the human passions of love, hate and intrigue which Home and Sophocles painted so clearly for us, suddenly drop into perspective. I don't think it can possibly be otherwise in a land where so much living has taken place.

The Treasury of Atreus, or Tomb of Agamemnon (as the guidebooks call it now), certainly dates from his time. It is of a beehive shape, and one is struck by the similarity to build-ings that can be seen in the far-off ancient cities of Ceylon, but which were of a slightly later period. No treasures were found in the tomb, for it was 'discovered' a lot earlier by graverobbers and the valuables removed to the 'safe place' of their pockets. Well, perhaps they needed the money. Nine of these beehive tombs were discovered, and a nearby one is named the Tomb of Clytemnestra.

The best time to visit Epidaurus is at the time of the festival in high summer. Then, the ancient plays are performed in the great open-air theatre which possesses such magnificent acoustic properties that a pin dropped in the central area can be heard at the top row of the 'gallery'. The background of dark trees and a wide sky are magical and even if you do not understand one word of Greek it will not matter a bit. Texts are provided in English, French and German, but it is the setting and the atmosphere which are the reason for going to this site.

Epidaurus was another of the city states of antiquity. The inhabitants practiced the cult of Asklepios, which came to the area from Thessaly, but the Epidaureans altered the myth to maintain that the god had been born in their district. Asklepios, fruit of a union between Apollo and a mortal woman, was given into the care of a Centaur for his upbringing. The Centaurs were considered to be the wisest of all creatures, and one of the great gifts that Asclepios is said to have possessed was that of healing. His father, the sun god, was said to have the same quality. Habits die hard. We, with all our modern learning, incline to the belief that sunshine is good for everything.

The worship of Asklepios grew greatly after the terrible plagues which swept the land during the Peloponnesian Wars, and Athenians officially adopted the cult in 420 B.C. Epidaurus became the most important centre (even surpassing the island of Kos, birthplace of Hippocrates, father of medicine) and, in time a festival was established called the Asklepieia. It started as an athletic festival, but later included 'musical' contests. This did not mean musical as we use the term, but rather contests of an intellectual nature. Hence the present form of the festivals in the ancient theatre, restarted in 1954.

In the beginning, the worship of the healer god took the form of sacrifices, washing ceremonies, and sleep. The last named took place in a special building, where the patient would be visited in a dream by the god who would advise on the form treatment should take. This usually included the horrid practice of allowing sacred snakes to lick the afflicted part. Later the practices changed into a kind of sanatorium where exercise, diet and drugs could be given, but they were far from the institutions offering these things that we know today. They could be compared more to the miracle centres of Lourdes in France, or Tinos in Greece. Patients paid according to their means, but it was very unlucky not to offer payment. (I wonder who started *that* belief!) Women in labour were not allowed to the sanctuary, and neither were those *in extremis,* so they were all put into nearby guest houses. These, in fact, were the forerunners of hospitals, and their foundations still remain.

Again this is a site which needs more time, particularly if

you are interested in the history of medicine. The museum is particularly good of its kind, with beautiful mosaics and statues and many fragments from the temples and other buildings which housed the sick and hopeless. One visits so many places where war is the main theme. Epidaurus has a compassion, and therefore exudes a quite different atmosphere to others visited in the one day excursion.

A few miles further on is Nauplion. This rather pleasant little town, sitting on a hillside overlooking the sea, was supposedly founded by Nauplius, whose only claim to fame as far as I can ascertain, is that he invented arithmetic and the alphabet, so I'm not sure that schoolchildren would be very happy to honour him. But Nauplion had its own moment of glory, for it was the first capital of the emergent Greek nation after the War of Independence before the parliament and the king elected to move to Athens. There are several hotels where lunch can be obtained, and there is a marvellous view of the Venetian fort which picturesquely sits in the bay. Disappointingly it turns out to be a hotel now.

The very nicest way to arrive at Delphi is by sea to Itea, and then to persuade a taxidriver to take you up the long mountainside to the new village of Delphi and then on to the famous site. The second, and more usual, is to drive out from Athens, past the orange groves and the honey beehives and the olive trees and across the fertile, but rather dull Boetian plain. Levadia is a nice little town where the tourist buses frequently stop in the lower streets. The road northwards goes to Lamia via Chaironeia, where Philip of Macedonia fought and won against the armies of southern Greece, and where, less than 300 years later, Roman Sulla in his turn established supremacy.

To the south, if we had time, we would find the Byzantine remains of the monastery of Osios Loukas, and, too, hear the echoes of the Second World War at Dhistomo which felt the weight of Nazi reprisals. But we go onwards, past the Triple Way, where Oedipus is said to have murdered his father, and follow the Sacred Way into the defile between the mountains where the rocks are piled, one upon another as if hurled in some Cyclopean game of bowls. This is stark, stern landscape, and it is no wonder that it instilled foreboding into the hearts of the simple peoples who first dwelt in these areas. Mountain folk are superstitious at the best of times. They live too close to Nature to be otherwise, and here one can really imagine that one lives in the presence of the Shining Ones.

The road curves up and around the lower slope of Mount Parnassus to Arakhova, where the wine is good, the girls pretty and the tourist orientated rugs and embroidery brighten the facades of the village houses, while the view across the wide breast of Pleiston Gorge is beautiful beyond belief. Then, it starts to descend.

Arrival at the 'Navel of the Earth' is almost by accident. It cannot be missed because inevitably there is an untidy sprawl of tourist traffic long before one arrives, wedging itself into minute spaces along the rock face or occupying half the narrow roadway, or jaywalking happily in front of the cars, so there is little room to pass. If you come to Delphi by tourist bus, there is no problem, but with a car, be prepared to have to leave it some way from the site itself. I prefer to do that in any case, because then the Oracle is approached properly — on foot.

On the right, lower than the road, is the Sanctuary of Athena Pronaia, where the remains of the Tholos are among the most beautiful in Delphi. This is also the area of the Gymnasium. Built during the 4th century B.C. and restored extensively during Roman times, it was used for the exercise and training of athletes entering the Pythian Games, and the remains of hot and cold baths can still be seen as well as the wrestling area. This is a particularly photogenic ruin, and the custodians are always a 'chatty' lot, pointing out the best places to stand. Maybe they get less visitors than the main ruins because it does take a little of the agility of a goat to scramble up and down the slopes from the roadway, but once there, one is inclined to linger and then the little stout man with the peaked cap fills one's ears with stories of the past in the most delightfully fractured English. He does not expect drachma for his pains, but he earns anything he gets.

On the opposite side of the main road, where the rocks of the Phaedriades loom over the road, is the Castalian spring. It was here that Apollo was said to have planted a laurel tree, ever after the symbol of victory, and it was at this spring that the faithful purified themselves in readiness for the rites at Delphi. The water was channelled through a fountain and gushed from the mouths of seven lions, but today only the holes in the rock, and the carved hollows which served as niches for offerings to the nymph Castella, are left. We, sadly, must remain among the great unwashed.

Just how ancient are the legends of Delphi one can only guess, but it is presumed that the spot became sacred originally due to mysterious 'exhalations' from a cave. At first associated with the earth goddess, the cults later switched to the worship of Apollo in the shape of a dolphin. Thus, from the Greek *delphos,* came the name Delphi. To the ancients, Apollo was heard through the voice of Pythia, an aged woman. To approach her to ask for an oracle or pronouncement, a supplicant had to pay a fee called a *pelanos,* wash at the Castalian fountain and sacrifice to the god. Pythia then disappeared into the room in the temple where the tripod stood, chewed laurel leaves and drank water. Then she sat on the tripod, breathed in the vapour from the hole in the ground, fell into a trance, heard a loud voice from within the *oikos,* and in turn answered it. The resultant phrases, sometimes making no sense at all, were then interpreted by the priests.

The ancients gave great credence to the oracle, obeying its 'orders' implicitly. Its power spread far beyond the boundaries of Greece and foreign powers sent much wéalth to the sanctuary. You can see the buildings of these treasuries still on the sides of the hill on which Delphi climbs, along the winding course of the Sacred Way. It was not until the coming of Sulla that the power of the oracle waned, finally falling into disuse completely with the coming of Christianity. The most famous oracle of all must surely be 'Tell the king the fairwrought hall has fallen to the ground. No longer has Phoebus a hut nor a prophetic laurel, nor a spring that speaks. The water of speech even is quenched.'

She spoke more truly than she could possibly have fore-seen. Temples, laurels, fountains, even houses are gone. The old village was removed in order to excavate ancient Delphi (for which the French paid most generously). Yet the magic remains, and the drawing power too, just as in those far-off ages, as thousands come to see this, one of the most impressive and fascinatingly beautiful places in the world.

Before leaving Delphi, make time to visit the Museum. It is not the most attractive of buildings but its most famous inmate is the bronze charioteer, ex-voto of the Prince Polyzalos of Sicily, who won a chariot race in the Pythian Games in 478 B.C., but there are also many other arresting pieces. There is Antinous, Hadrian's favourite, a marble statue of a little girl, who smiles for all eternity, and there is a small boy, clasping a goose, for all the world like a piece of Lladro porcelain.

Athens is excellently placed for many excursions and early one spring morning, we presented ourselves at the closed facade of a small *periptero* in Amalias Avenue, along with half a dozen other assorted humans, who, from the prodigiousness of their yawns, had been equally reluctant to leave warm beds for a wait on a cold pavement. We were all bound for a day's cruise among the islands of the Saronic Gulf, visiting Hydra, Aegina and Poros. I had been to Hydra before, but the chance of a day at sea in the bone-warming sunshine of Greek April, and with a little sortie to the islands had been too good to miss. The other passengers were a mixed bag, mostly American and German, but with a sprinkling of French and a *soupçon* of British and/or Australians, usually scooped together for identification in Greece as locals just cannot tell them apart.

The coach took us to Zea Marina, where we boarded the *Saronic Star,* a pleasant little vessel which is a scaled-down version of her big cruise sisters, with a small bar and dining room, but I waited until we arrived in Hydra for my coffee. There are so many charming little cafes strung along its attractive, if somewhat arty, waterfront. The town reminds me in some ways of St Tropez about 25 years ago, before the cataclysmic advent of 'B.B.' I do hope it will not be changed now that so many summer visitors go there, for it has a friendly and informal manner with its donkeys, its little tourist shops and its fisher families spread along the harbour walls, patiently mending nets. The rocky island of Hydra has no cars and no water, but it has a seafaring tradition which is second to none in Greece. The town consists of tall nineteenth-century mansions belonging to many merchant families who made their money in the Greek maritime fleets and who, during the War of Independence, gave a great deal to the cause. The families had originally come to Hydra when Turkish oppression forced them to flee from Epirus. They had turned to the sea for a living, built fine houses against the inhospitable rock face, each with its own storerooms and water cisterns and, used to a piratical outlook, ran the British blockade during the Napoleonic Wars, making individual fortunes in the process. With their anti-Turkish outlook, they were only too happy to throw in their lot with the Revolutionaries, supplying ships and men, under two leaders, Tombazis and Miaoulis.

When the island lost its importance as a maritime base, it turned to tourism and, I think, probably does even better out of that. There are lots of good little shops, including the ever courteous 'The House of Greek Art' run by Adreades, but my day was made by the discovery of two leather-faced solemn-looking sponge sellers along the harbour. Having sorted out the essential preliminaries of whether I was 'Inglise/Amerkain' and having succeeded in bribing them to pose for me, a happy bargain was struck over several excellent sponges. I have no doubt at all that they made the money up on a more trusting soul later in the day. I would recommend that you try to spend a day in Hydra, more if you have time or are interested in the arts, for the Athens School of Fine Arts is accommodated in the impressive Tombazis mansion. But avoid high summer, the town gets so crowded and hot and there are no beaches to speak of. Make the journey in spring or early autumn and you will enjoy every moment.

Aegina is quite different. An almost picture-postcard mountain of the shape drawn by children, slopes down to the Saronic Gulf, providing an attractive view from most beaches in the vicinity of Athens. Aegina too has its roots in history. Because of the wealth derived from its shipping and its ceramic industries, it rivalled Athens in power at one time, but it dwindled away into nothingness, despite the majestic ruins of the Temple of Aphaea perched high above the little town of Aghia Marina. Now it is a popular holiday spot for Athenians and has a few pleasant hotels, so it has the disadvantage of drawing too many people at weekends, thus losing the quality of remoteness which is the main attraction of most Greek islands. There are some nice little shops above the harbour, some with exquisite hand embroidery, which the girls make, along with all the woollen articles they sell, during the winter months. But they told me that it is getting more and more difficult to obtain the fine Irish linen on which they prefer to work.

Poros needs to be seen in sunlight, or it can be a little disappointing after the sophistication of Hydra and the prettiness of Aegina. The best thing, apart from the narrow strait which divides the town from Galata and the consequent liveliness of the traffic to and fro, is the splendid view of the mainland. In fact it is only the town, built on the headland, which is called Poros, but an isthmus joins it to Kalavria and the whole goes under the name of Poros. There are the remnants of a temple to Poseidon and of an old sanctuary, but it is really the present-day atmosphere which is the attraction. It is all very relaxing and exceedingly, splendidly Greek, so that the two-seater bicycles pounced upon by the tourists all look a little out of place.

6 Tips for Tourists

The claim that Delphi was the centre of the earth in ancient times, could still be made today by the whole of this part of Greece, for one look at the position of Athens on a world map shows that she is beautifully poised between the land masses of Europe and the Near East. But the overland journeys, despite modern transport, are still long to modern eyes used to crossing the universe in hours. It takes several days by coach or car or rail across Europe. Sea routes, too, take a little while, although there are many regular shipping and ferry lines linking Piraeus with foreign ports all round the Mediterranean and Adriatic

With the limited time at the disposal of most holidaymakers, it is natural that the majority of visitors from Northern Europe come by air. At least 17 foreign airlines fly into Athens on scheduled and charter flights. They land at the Eastern Airport, but the national airline of Greece, Olympic Airways, flies all its services, both domestic and international, from Western Airport. Both sections are at Ellenikon on the coast north of Glyfada, and there are regular bus services into the terminals in the city.

The airport terminals in Syngrou seem at the end of the earth on a very hot August afternoon, particularly if laden with suitcases, and waiting dustily and hopefully at the kerbside. Eventually a taxi will heave itself into view, with the driver looking as if he has just fallen out of bed. But don't let that fool you, because it's an illusion to reassure the tourist. Once you are esconced in the back seat all sleep immediately departs his eyes, behind his sunglasses, and he is galvanised into action as if pursued by the Furies themselves.

It is not just for decoration that the front compartment of an Athens taxi is festooned with religious ikons, worry beads, pictures of his family and plastic flowers. They are all there as morale boosters and to invoke heavenly protection against other drivers, and the shouts, armwaving and even banging on the side panels of the unfortunate cab are calculated to play safe and drive away all possible demons, while your driver takes shortcuts in congested, impossibly narrow lanes, thrusts across traffic streams, and appeals to every passerby to witness the stupidity of the rest of humanity. At the same time, if you have an English-speaking one, he will probably be holding some conversation with you, congratulating you if you are English, commiserating if you are neither English nor Greek, and expressing his opinion of world politics as a whole. This, I must add in fairness, I found to be the case whoever was in power in Greece. It takes more than a few colonels to stop the flow of an Athens taxi driver in full flood!

I happened also to be in Athens at the time of the American presidential elections, and the wholesale delight at the discomfiture of Nixon was expressed in uninhibited terms by no less than three different cabbies. . . . One certainly gets a picture of a typical 'man in a taxi' on journeys like these. The only time that an Athens driver is comparatively silent is when it rains. I have come to the conclusion that both vehicle and driver hate wet weather as much as a backyard moggy does, for most of them vanish from view. The ones that do stay on duty, and that you can persuade to stop for you, seem to have lost the use of their horns and tongues with the disappearance of the sun and sit glumly in the incessant traffic jams with their two-way radios crackling with indignation. The fare structures are supposed to stay stable, but in wet weather journeys seem to get more expensive and take longer.

Occasionally it happens that a taxi, already engaged, will stop, ask where you are going, and you share the fare with the sitting tenant. I am not sure that it is legal, but it happens, and then one has most interesting, and often very useful and enlightening conversations with all occupants at once. Officially, there is a flat rate charge upon hire, and then a charge per kilometre within Athens. Beyond the perimeter, the fares are approximately doubled. Higher rates apply at midnight, and at Christmas and Easter.

I must admit to a love/hate relationship with Athens taxis. I'll never forget one afternoon in Phaleron when I was stricken with toothache and hailed a prowling cab and asked the driver to find a pharmacy. He ran one to earth, in the middle of the siesta hours in Piraeus, and on the way back, stopped the cab beside the wall of someone's garden. It was covered with beautiful blue jasmine, and my driver hopped out, picked a huge spray of the perfumed flowers and with a flourish said in the best English he could muster, 'For you lady, because you have pain in your mouth'. How could one possibly dislike a breed of men who produce gems like that? But one can when driving for oneself, and they are then the opposition!

Most cities have their own individual set of traffic problems. Athens must be high on any list of the world's worst for visiting drivers. The combination of grossly overcrowded, narrow roads, meant for the horse and cart and never for four-lane motor traffic, totally incomprehensible road signs, hidden away high on the sides of buildings, often almost obscured by generations of dust, and road users who are for the most part totally oblivious to the requirements of other drivers and seemingly hell bent on personal and universal destruction, can only be matched by the driving patterns in Tokyo and Bangkok. I have never quite been able to understand this quirk in Greek natures. After all, although they are highly emotional, volatile people, most Greeks are also exceedingly courteous and charming, seldom given to aggression to strangers. Yet put them behind the wheel of a car and they change like the two masks of Comedy and Tragedy. Granted they cannot know that one is a stranger in their midst if driving a hirecar with a local registration, so for some years now I have affixed a Union Jack sticker fore and aft on all the wheeled transport I use. It certainly helps other drivers to identify the crazy foreigner and hopefully give her a wide berth and, equally important, it helps to identify the strange vehicle if one has forgotten the number and it is not written on the car key. I strongly recommend you to do the same in Athens. It helps at least to get a smile and a wave as they crowd one round a corner on two wheels!

It also helps with parking, for again in common with other cities, the problems attendant on finding space are legion. There are a number of car parks especially for tourists (re-check on their positions when you visit) and there is a garage park near Syntagma, as well as a number of open parking spaces on building sites, which also change from time to time. One gives the keys to the attendant and he parks the vehicle. There are also meter areas, including a large one by the cathedral, but it is not easy to get in there, except later in the evening. If one parks in a no-parking area, Athenian police are sometimes patient, but they also often remove number plates, which can then entail a trip to the police station to retrieve them, a fine and a lecture on one's shortcomings as a citizen. I came back to my hired vehicle one day to find a policeman busily engaged in this original practice, but when he realised I was a visitor, he let me off, while wagging his finger and saying 'No parking' in English, German, French and Greek to make sure I comprehended! Then, the sticker helped, but for how long can luck hold?

There are a number of reputable car hire firms in Athens, such as Hellascars, Byron Car Hire, Europcar, Avis and Hertz. There are smaller ones too, but good as they may be, and cheaper as they undoubtedly are, I would advise you to stick to the company whose contract is written in English as well as Greek. Otherwise you cannot read the small print, and in the event of accidents, this can become an expensive business.

Fly/drive packages are usually worth considering if you intend to travel around within a certain area, as they save wear and tear on your own transport, but if you have the time and inclination to drive the long dusty road from 'wherever' with your own car, make sure that your insurances are valid for Greece, use an international or a British driving licence, and remember to collect your tourist petrol coupons at border points and ports, or at certain banks. They save approximately 40% on pump prices. Driving is on the right (more or less!) and priority is always on the right. The road signs do appear in most cases in both the Greek and Latin alphabet, but spellings differ greatly so slow down sufficiently to decipher them. Speed limits are enforced, although one might not think so at first sight, and as you are sure to be the one to be caught, take care. The Greek Automobile Club (ELPA) has efficient little yellow vans marked Assistance Routière, and give free assistance to foreigners. On the spot repairs are also free, but spare parts are charged as per ELPA's price list. Apart from their welcome little yellow perils, ELPA will also come in response to a telephone call (in or around Athens telephone 604411).

With all the difficulties attendant on driving within the perimeters of Athens you may prefer to use local buses. If so, I strongly recommend that you try to avoid the rush hour, but apart from that the bus services are easy and quite plentiful, though the vehicles are not always in pristine condition. There are about 40 bus and trolley routes in Athens and its vicinity, and most come to or near Omonia and Syntagma Squares, the twin hearts of the city. Bus stops are differently coloured. Blue for buses and yellow for trolley buses and are marked 'Stasis' (the 'S' in the Greek language looks like an 'M' on its side) and you must always remember that the many one-way systems in operation will affect your descent point on the return journey, so take advice from the other passengers. They will tell you at once — in concert! The vehicles are numbered but if you prefer to read destination boards you will have to get a working knowledge of the Greek alphabet or learn to recognise the ones you want. Fares are standardised in central Athens, but it is useless to quote them here, as they, like others elsewhere, are subject to change. They are not expensive by British standards. The system is to enter by the rear doors, and leave by the front, but that seldom works in practice in rush hour when getting on is a major achievement let alone struggling through the mass of bodies. A list of the main bus routes, both within the city and to the suburbs will be found at the end of this chapter. Long distance buses have their own terminals, and details of these will also be found at the end of the chapter.

I think I must point out that long distance buses are not always up to Green Line or Greyhound standard, although they have improved greatly in recent years. It may be that I always seem to be blessed with a seat-sharing passenger, who, whether male or female, is twice my size and is firmly ensconced before my arrival so that I spend my travelling time perched on a narrow ledge like a budgie. You may be luckier. But there is no better way to get in close proximity (in more ways than one!) with your Greek hosts, for people are very friendly when going about their every day business and travelling to and from their work and family homes, and all of them, priests and all, mixed up with an assortment of baggage that would frighten even the average English country bus into a paroxysm. When waiting for any bus in Greece, let alone Athens, there is no question of an orderly queue, so apart from inflicting actual bodily injury, it's a case of each man for himself.

Similar comments apply to the ferries between Piraeus and the islands in the Saronic Gulf, which are almost to be considered Athenian suburbs. Aegina particularly qualifies and there are no less than 24 weekday sailings, increased to 33 at weekends. There is no ceremony on these ferries, but they have an advantage over buses because they allow one to stretch one's legs in the open air, and of course to enjoy the little opportunity of crossing a small stretch of the precious blue sea. Incidentally it is not always blue. It can change to palest almond, or slate grey, and although it looks pretty clean, these waters are polluted. There are now considerable efforts to clean them up, if only to keep the tourist image untarnished, but it is not easy to repair the careless ravages of generations. At the islands the position is far better than in the close vicinity of Athens and Piraeus, and many Athenians go out to them at weekends for their beach sorties. You will seldom see Greeks actually in the water before June. They leave that to the sun-starved Northerners to whom one wink of reflected light across the surface of the sea is enough to send them rushing lemming like towards it, discarding their furs the while!

Local ferry fares are reasonable, and with plenty of time at your disposal you could visit several of the islands, taking a day at each, returning to Athens at night or next day. But with less time to spare, it is worth taking a one-day cruise from Zea Marina, visiting Aegina, Hydra and usually Poros, before returning to the mainland in early evening. Transfers, lunch and taxes are included in the fares, and the ships are very comfortable scaled down versions of their bigger brethren. As most of the passengers are tourists, one does miss 'local' atmosphere except on the islands themselves and there is not much time to find this either, but it is an extremely pleasant and relaxing day. You will find a few details of the places mentioned in the Excursion chapter, so that you can use them in whichever way you may require.

Returning from ferries to the centre of Piraeus, the one 'Underground' route is a convenient way of getting back into Athens. It is not strictly 'underground' of course, except in the central section and it should be asked for as Electrikos, or as Metro. There are about 18 stations on this privately owned little line which runs in a north south direction between Piraeus and the suburb of Kifissia, via Athens. The whole journey takes about 40 minutes, but from Piraeus it takes about 25 minutes to reach Omonia. The service operates regularly between 5.30 am to 15 minutes past midnight, which makes it a most useful system for the cruise passenger who prefers to go under his own steam rather than on an organised sightseeing tour. The most interesting section, for the historian at least, is the little piece between Thesion and Monastiraki. This runs alongside the Agora and virtually over the past, for when the line was being laid, remnants of classical Greece, part of the Panathenaic Way and of the old Turkish town, were found . . . and lost.

I have been trying to draw together a few facts on the hotels in

Athens which might be useful to readers, and it occurs to me that if Byron had visited modern Athens he might never have become famous. Certainly the opportunities for accommodation for visitors, have come a long way from the little house where a widow and a daughter offered genteel lodgings. Byron is unlikely to have written the 'Maid of Athens' about the swarms of waiters, housemaids and bellhops who draw their daily bread from the enormous presentday industry. On occasion, service can be slow enough to have allowed him the time ... but that is a hazard not confined to Greece. In compensation, service is almost universally courteous, and willing. Two examples will illustrate.

After a considerable delay in getting away from Gatwick one January day, two of us arrived at the Astir Palace Hotel at Vouliagmeni late at night. We had telexed ahead to explain our tardiness, but were surprised to be met by the manager himself, sweeping away apologies, and saying that a meal would be waiting for us after our long and tiring journey. We washed away our weariness, and went down to the huge diningroom. Apart from ourselves, there was not a guest to be seen, but every candle was lit, a little chorus line of cheerful waiters stood by, and the pianist, nodding and smiling in our direction, played as long as we stayed to listen. The hotel could easily have explained that it was winter, and that the dining room was closed early and we could have had a light meal in our room, but that would not have been the service they prided themselves on. On another occasion, in early spring, I was staying at a very small hotel in the centre of Athens and on my first appearance into the little dining room, I confounded the waiter by asking for lemon with my tea. He rushed off behind his green baize door, appeared moments later donning his outdoor jacket and hurtled out of the front door of the hotel. I waited. Sure enough, he returned some while later, clutching a paper bag, and within a few minutes, I was triumphantly presented with my pot of tea, and a neatly sliced whole lemon. To me those examples more than make up for the in-season irritations when there are just too many people to deal with, for they prove that, given the opportunity, service still exists in Athens.

This city has always been used to visitors, but it is only in the last 20 years that the influx of peaceful invaders has been on such a gigantic scale. Consequently and with few exceptions, the hotels are mostly modern, well equipped and efficient. In view of general world inflation they are also, for the most part, reasonably priced, particularly if one is staying under a package tour deal. It is better to take half-pension rather than full. This allows more flexibility in trying out some of the local eating places for the evening meal, or for being away all day on an excursion. Even within Athens it is irritating to have to trail all the way back to the hotel for a meal when enticing smells waft from a nearby taverna or from the endless open booths. In winter it is not *so* difficult to find hotel accommodation, but in high season it is advisable to book ahead. Lists of hotels of all grades can be obtained through Tourist Offices, but I am enclosing a brief comment here on what to expect in those grades, and a few names of the better known premises which might be a useful pointer for prospective travellers.

There are six grades in the hotel category system used in Greece: Luxury (L) A, B, C, D, E. In the categories A to E, there is a framework of fixed prices, and hotels are only allowed to charge up to the top rate within the category designated to them. Prices of luxury hotels, however, and first class hotel suites, are fixed at the discretion of the establishment themselves, but in most cases they are not excessive when compared to similar standards elsewhere. All rooms in L and A, the majority in B and some in C have private shower or bath facilities. In D private baths and toilets are seldom found, but most of these humbler premises are clean and welcoming. I cannot always say the same for E grades. Perhaps I am not adventurous when it comes to hotel experimentation.

In category A, there are also a growing number of apartment complexes in the vicinity of Athens and these are ideal for the do-as-you-please people, or those who have special dietary requirements. Youth hostel and camping site standards conform to those found elsewhere across Europe. The youth hostel in Athens at Kipseli, the YMCA (XEN) at Omirou and the YWCA (XAN) at Amerikis are always full to the ceiling with an international guest list and offer exceptional value for money, but there are no frills of any kind. The nearest camping site is Athens Camping, at Peristeri on the Dafni road. It is open all year but, like Dafni Camping, beside the old monastery, and some 10 kilometres from Athens (open July/September) it gets decidedly like a rugby scrum in high season. My personal choice would be to go further out of Athens and commute. There is a pleasant little site at Voula, some 20 kms from Athens, open in summer only, which has the advantage of good sea bathing. If you do not want a camping site, have no bookings, and can't find your own accommodation, ask the Tourist Police to aid you. Don't be put off by the name. They are a completely non-political body and will help in every way possible. (Emergency No. 171).

Probably the best known hotel in Athens is the Grande Bretagne on Syntagma Square. Once a private mansion, and then headquarters for the Allies for a period at the end of the Second World War, it still remains one of the most elegant, and attractive among its fellow hotels, and service, although on the slow side, is as impeccable and stately as one might expect. King George, next door, is only slightly less grand, and if unfamiliar with the two hotels, one can get muddled between their facades, so look at the names before galloping up the steps to meet someone. It is a little disconcerting to have to rush out into the streets and up the next flight . . . I know. I have succeeded in making the mistake twice!

Other luxury hotels are Amalia, Kings Palace, Athene Palace, Athens Hilton, Caravel, Royal Olympic and the gently elegant Acropole Palace, which is opposite the National Museum in Patission. First class and reliable are Grand Minos, Olympic Palace, Ambassadors, Attica Palace, and Electra, and they are now joined by the Athens Chandris on Syngrou, a welcome addition on the airport side of the city, useful if one has one's own transport. Then there are the rash of hotels widely used by package tour operators in category B, such as Stanley, El Greco, Plaka, Aretoussa, Marmara Atlantic and, coming more and more into the popularity charts, the self-catering flats already mentioned. They can usually be rented by the week and a few of the better ones are, Delice, Ariana, Embassy, Priomos, and Ava.

Many people prefer to stay in the coastal suburbs rather than in central Athens, as it is always slightly cooler in summer, but this depends on what you are intending to do during your stay, and how much time you are prepared to spend on travelling. There are a number of hotels in the Piraeus area which covers Microlimano, Kastella and New Phaliron, all in the B and C class, and although I cannot speak from personal experience, they look as though they may well give one value for money as well as an authentic Greek atmosphere. Glyfada, further down the coast, is the most popular with Athenians as well as tourists, despite constant airport noise. I like this little place very much, with its marinas, its tavernas, its little pub, and very pleasant small shops which are well used to foreigner's sign language and make allowances for them. Many package tours use Glyphada (or Glyfada) as their base and among the hotels are Florida, Gripsholm and Antonopoulos. Look for the remains of an early Christian basilica near the last named. It is said that St Paul landed on Greek soil at this point. The First Tourist, indeed. . . . A little further along are the Astir Bungalows, well equipped in the luxury class, with their own beach and a good restaurant. They make a pleasant base from which to explore the Attican peninsula or to get into central Athens on the regular bus route.

All the way to Sounion, along the undulating, beautiful coastline, there are an assortment of hotels, and service flats, as well as Athenians' summer homes. Among the hotels, I have two favourites. The Astir Palace, already mentioned, and the National Tourist Organisation's Xenia Hotel at Lagonissi, which has a equally delightful situation. The latter is better as a holiday hotel than as a base for exploring Athens, but it might provide a useful change of venue if

August Athens gets too much to take. All the coastal hotels should be booked in advance; they are popular with local people as well as tourists. The same remark applies to Kifissia, the cool suburb north of Athens, where there are a few pleasant hotels and restaurants.

'Greek Food is either very good or very bad. There is no in-between.' A somewhat sweeping statement but it is not so far from the truth. There is no great cuisine in Greece, so enjoyment depends to a great extent on the freshness of the dishes served, and as in very many instances the fish or meat is cooked as the customer demands, one can usually rely on a pleasant meal. It is seldom expensive by our standards, though prices have increased considerably in recent years. It is also rather fattening despite the constant salad offerings, mainly because of the oil content. It also suffers from an almost universal inability to get to the table in a hot condition. Make up your mind that everything you order is likely to arrive tepid, and you will not be disappointed, and may even be pleasantly surprised.

Despite the absence of haute cuisine, there are very many specialities, most of which appeal to our palates, and before going on to the subject of where to eat them, it might be useful to have an idea of what they are. It is usual to order an aperitif. This will probably be ouzo, which is very similar to Pernod (a colourless liquid to which, if you are wise, you add water unless you are accustomed to strong drink and its sudden effect). With the aperitifs you may order, or in many places you will be offered without ordering, *mezedes.* These are small titbits such as cheese of the local variety called *feta,* olives, small sausages called *loukanika, tiropitakia,* which is a miniature cheese pie, *dolmadakia,* the very attractive little vine leaves rolled around rice fillings, and many more. The choice is endless and depends on the inspiration or lack of it, of the taverna proprietor. Some of the dishes served will appear again in the main courses, and if one is extra fond of them, that is the better way to order. For me, *taramosalata,* which is grey mullet roe pounded into a creamy paste, shrimps, (or *garides*) octopus, *tsatsiki,* a thick savoury yoghourt, are always in this category. In some tavernas a complete meal can be ordered in the form of *mezedes*. One particular instance of this is at Vassilenas, at Piraeus, where you do not have any choice in the matter, because the proprietor dreams up the dishes for you and about 20 of them appear *before* the main dishes, all for an inclusive price. The big problem about eating at Vassilenas is that you feel obliged to eat everything, for fear of disappointing the chef . . . and no one that I know can eat that much!

For the main meal, it is advisable to stick to lamb, pork or chicken, rather than beef or veal (often on the tough side). Minced meat of course is better, and this is found in the famous *moussaka*, which also contains aubergines and cheese, and which *can* be the most splendid dish in the world . . . or the worst, dependant on your luck with the chef! Fish is plentiful but always expensive. One has to remember that the Aegean is as fished-out as many other waters these days, and the fishermen do not have an easy time. *Barbounia*, which is red mullet, is delicious, and so is *xifias* (swordfish). If you like whitebait, ask for *marides*, and if you like fish stews, known as *kakavia*, go to the Piraeus restaurants, particularly the Melissa on Akti Poseidonos. It is a rather scruffy, steamy little place, a real 'Joe's joint' with marble-topped tables, but all the locals go there at lunchtime, the food is hot, excellent, and very reasonably priced. Do not bother with shellfish, unless you are eating on expense accounts. Finally, do not forget *souvlakia*, whose other name will probably be more familiar— shish kebab, the well-known pieces of meat and liver, onion and tomato, skewered together and grilled.

So many dishes in Greece have Turkish origins, and Turkish names. One cannot go through centuries of occupation without many habits rubbing off. The aforementioned *feta*, local white cheese found always in the delicious and inevitable salads, is a case in point, and many of the most beloved among Greek sweets are also given Turkish names and have their origins in the past. *Baclava*, a nut and pastry confection smothered in honey, or *kadaifi* (kataifi) which is a kind of honey-soaked shredded wheat, *galakto boureko*, a custard pie

—all owe their continued existence in Greece to that hated 500 years.

Incidentally, sweet courses are seldom served in tavernas. They usually stick to offerings of seasonal fruits, and if you particularly want a sweet, they send someone to the nearest pastry shop (*zakharoplasteion*) or you can go yourself to a *galaktopoleian* (milkbar, you will easily deduce that *galakto* refers to milk products). These milkbars serve light meals, coffee, milk, etc, and very often have *loukoumades,* delicious little honey-soaked fritters. You will not get beer in the milkbar, any more than you do in U.K. Icecream is usually good though, and you can ask for a glass of water. It is safe in Athens, but if you are still uncertain, buy Loutraki, which is the local spa bottled water and very pleasant.

Greek wines cannot be put into the 'exciting' class, but they are pleasant and go very well, as they are intended to, with Greek food. The better wines are Porto Carras, Chevalier du Rhodes, Naoussa (all reds) Demestica (known to all irreverent British as 'Domestos'), Cambas (red and white) and the delicious, but very sweet Samos, if you are drinking with your dessert course. Retsina, the resinated and most controversial of Greek wines, is a somewhat acquired taste. It is good with certain Greek dishes, but the turpentiny flavour is not, usually, beloved of foreigners. Raki is a stronger form of ouzo, and the brandy, Metaxas, is rougher than the French varieties, but is very good indeed, especially if taken with soda or ginger ale, etc. Local beers are pleasant, ask for Fix . . . not a shot of dope, but a long light cool beer, and less expensive than the imported varieties.

Where to eat all these things? Athens has thousands of eating places of all kinds from small cafes and open booths selling cheese pies and *souvlakia,* to restaurants. These are also in various categories and it is often difficult to know the difference between them and tavernas. The latter are usually less formal, and do not always open at lunchtime and also usually only supply food in Greek style, although these days one is finding Western food creeping in, more's the pity. The restaurant invariably has an international menu.

One can always study the menu pinned up outside to get an idea of cost and content, and it is usually written in several languages in tourist areas. There are literally dozens of tavernas in the Plaka and Kolonaki districts. Do not go to the first one you see but stroll up and down a bit and look to see which ones are busy, particularly with local clientele—a good sign in any country—and then, make your way directly to the back of the premises to the kitchen area to have a look at the bubbling cauldrons, and point to the things you want. If you do not see anything you fancy, ask for something from the cold cabinet. The patron will then open the doors of his fridge and produce trays of fish and meat for your inspection and you pick the size you want and pay accordingly. A very fair system I think you'll agree.

Among the restaurants, there are two in Kolonaki that I like, both for service and atmosphere, and taxi-drivers will know both. Gerofinikas, at 10, Pindarou, reached by a narrow alley entrance, is used by the 'upper-class Athenian', if I may use the expression, and Europa, with little Greek atmosphere, apart from the waiters, and a fascinating set of old prints and pictures of Athens and famous Athenians of recent eras. I spend as much time examining them as I do eating, and the food is always excellent.

In the Plaka it is almost impossible to recommend, but I know I am safe to do so with Xenou which has been in business for a very long time (in summer go through to the little courtyard at the back, and sooner or later the musicians will arrive, so do not go earlier than 9.30 pm) and also Platanos and the Three Brothers, both near the Tower of the Winds. But tavernas open and close . . . find your own. It's much more fun that way. Local people go out to special districts for special dishes. To Halandri for pork, to Piraeus and Microlimano for fish (and I include Rafina in that sortie too because I like the unpretentious fish tavernas on the way down to the ferry embarkation point), and to Vlachika and Vari for country dishes such as *dolmadakia avgoulemono,* large vine-leaves rolled around rice filling and covered with lemon and egg sauce, and especially for lamb.

The Vari tradition came about in a most unusual way. The district was for generations just grazing land for the sheep flocks. After the advent of the motorcar the lanes got more and more hazardous until one day, inevitably, a sheep was killed by a passing car. The shepherd decided that waste was a bad thing, so he lit a fire, roasted the carcass and offered the meat to passersby. The idea caught on, and in no time a series of stalls and tavernas sprang up along the roadside, all specialising in roast lamb, but using more orthodox ways of killing it. . . . Each of the premises has a butchers shop, and one goes first to this and selects the meat required; it is weighed and the cost given immediately. Then it is taken away, cooked and by the time you are halfway through your first bottle of Demestica returned to the table together with the inevitable and ample salad of olives, tomatoes, onions, cucumbers and *feta*, all in olive oil and herb dressing. The cost is little, the finesse even less, but it is fresh, clean, succulent and thoroughly enjoyable. The waiters do not always speak good English, but the last time I was there, my waiter was extremely fluent in an Americanised version. It came as no surprise to know that he had been living in the US, and was a steward in disguise, just helping out at home between ships! One gets a life story along with the service, one of the delights of Athens.

On the old Sounion road, inland, is Peania. Go out there one evening to the Kanakis Garden Restaurant. This is a very pleasant and popular rendezvous, particularly as Kanakis supplies wines from his own vineyards and the whole place is most attractive. More expensive than the usual tavernas, but worth the extra for the change of view, particularly if you have a car. You could go on 'spec' because there are plenty of other tavernas in the vicinity, but if you are set on visiting Kanakis, get someone to telephone a booking for you.

Microlimano is by far the most popular of the coastal strip resorts for small restaurants and tavernas and certainly the most expensive. Kanaris is good. Try shrimps in the pot . . . and hope that the patron will dance on the table for you, but it doesn't happen every day! Kokini, Varka, Zorbas, Zefiros and many more, all have good varieties of fishy dishes. The fried or stewed squid (*kalamarakias*) is always superb, and for cheaper varieties of the same food, with paper tablecloths and no yacht basin views, go up to the little tavernas on the higher road between Piraeus and Microlimano beyond the naval station. I cannot tell you their names for I can only find them in the dark! But I believe they sit within what is left of the wall towers, once part of the Wall of Konon. Most little tavernas are alike along the coasts of Greece. No frills, no fancy service, but invariably clean paper tablecloths, clean food and plenty of it, at reasonable cost.

'I'm going to Athens. Is there anything you want me to bring back with me?' was the substance of a telephone call I made to my daughter recently. 'Oh yes please. Would you bring me back two flocati rugs for my bedroom.' I came away from the telephone wishing I hadn't asked. Two rugs would take up most of my luggage space. However, a promise was a promise.

Perhaps I had better explain. They are the long haired shaggy woolly rugs, off white, or dyed in various colours, which are so very good tempered in everyday use. They are made on mainland Greece, many of them in a district several hundred miles north of Athens called Larissa, and although prices have risen very considerably over the past few years, they still represent a good buy . . . if you have the room to carry them! Prices do vary with quality and size, as well as from shop to shop, and one has to look around a bit.

I was coming back from the Plaka at about 9 pm, still rug-less, when I saw that Karamouslis was still open, though the owner showed every sign of being about to go home. Within ten minutes I'd bought two off-white rugs, got them packed, paid for, and was marching homeward with an unwieldy parcel. If I had not been limited for space, I would have bought an even bigger assortment, for the rugs are very attractive, particularly in large sizes. I would recommend you to stick to the shops which specialise in these items. Kara-mouslis have their own factory in Larissa, so if you are in the vicinity you could go there. But the showroom in

Mitreopolis has enough variety to satisfy even the most pernickety of customers, and they will send and package back to almost anywhere in the world. Two other excellent and reliable shops for carpeting are Dia Babouri, 56 Adrianou, and for handwoven, rather more expensive affairs, the ones made by the disabled and sold in the showroom of the National Welfare Organisation, 22 Voukourestiou Street, are made to order.

Of course, shopping is a universally loved pastime, undertaken by tourists and business visitors alike, and is not confined to the attentions of the female sex. Men are inveterate shoppers, and contrary to general female belief they do usually know exactly what they are looking for, which is the reason that so many little boutiques and 'exclusive' shops, spring up in the vicinity of the expensive hotels used by business visitors. Athens is exceedingly well equipped with these premises, both within the hotel shopping complexes and around the immediate vicinity of Syntagma Square, along Stadiou, and Venizelos, and in Kolonaki. Prices are naturally higher when overheads on smart premises have to be paid, but quality is usually reliable. Jewellery, always a popular choice for the 'lady of the house' is beautiful in Greece, and selection is quite wide, from the exquisite designs begun by the ancient goldsmiths and traditionally associated with Thessaloniki, and with the Byzantine age, to the modern and exceptionally expensive Zolotas designs found in Ilias Lalaounis on Panepistimiou. You can find examples of Zolotas in many of the showcases in hotel vestibules, but for the traditional designs almost any of the goldsmith shops will provide standard selections. Do not pay the first, or the second, or even the third price asked. Just keep going! For pretty and inexpensive items not involving larger sums of money, there is a wide choice. Stalactite in Adrianou, is typical of many good small shops. But do not try to buy expensive items off street merchants, and certainly not at knockdown prices. . . . They have all been working in the business a lot longer than the visitors!

Koumboloi (worry beads), perhaps the most popular

souvenir, and one of the least expensive, *can* be bought from the street traders, from the *periptero,* from shops large and small, in fact, everywhere. They have, however, a shop of their very own, called Koumboloi Boutique (what else would it be called!) at Zalakosta Street. I have carried the olive beads in my handbag for years, but it was only recently that I sent several strings in various colours to a most unlikely destination. They were sent to a longhouse in the jungles of Sarawak, as a small 'thankyou' to the Ibans who had looked after me, and who love beads more than most things. I like to think of them adorning a bamboo leaf wall!

Handwoven shoulder bags, skirts, shirts, ceramics, dolls, can be found almost anywhere in Athens, but you could look first in the National Organisation of Handicrafts in Mitreopolis, because their designs are authentic. I have mentioned the Flea Market elsewhere, but this is certainly a place which deserves several visits. Go for fun on Sundays, and shop seriously on other days. Look for brasses, copper pans, icons, coffee pots, but do remember that genuine antiques require special licences for export, so anything offered without licence is immediately suspect. Papageorgious in Ifestou is well stocked for many less valuable pieces, so is Moschos and Frida. Take a look at the long meat skewers if you are a barbecue lover. They are reasonably priced and beautifully made.

For leather and fur goods, Athens can offer a surprising variety. The best of the fur shops are also around Syntagma, Ermou and Mitreopolis, and cleverly worked berets, cravats etc, made of many small pieces, are not expensive. Better skins obviously cost more, but it is worth investigating if you are a serious purchaser. I have long given up taking expensive items home. The house is already too full of souvenirs, so I content myself with pistachio nuts, herbs, figs, glacé fruits, honey, olive oil, and the like. Prices vary even in these, but they are so delicious when one gets back home and the sunny hillsides of Greece are a long way away.

General shopping hours vary with the seasons, but almost universally there is a complete closing for some hours in the afternoon. Check up at the hotel. Banks incidentally are open in the mornings and in the evenings for two hours between 17.30 and 19.30, and as they give so much better exchange rates than the hotels do make a note of them rather than be caught out.

By the time you have trotted around the shopping areas, the idea of a cup of coffee and a long sit watching the world go by is a most attractive proposition. Athens is well-equipped for this particular form of entertainment, and indeed, it is the primary occupation for Athenians, both in winter and summer, although in the colder days, much is viewed from the shelter of the cafes themselves. But in summer there is really nothing pleasanter than the pavement cafes, and you can find these all over the city.

The more expensive ones naturally have the best 'floor-show' and there are two types: 'tourist floorshow', and 'local floorshow'. The former is in Syntagma and the latter in Kolonaki. Omonia does not have that many, and it is rather too noisy and dirty in any case. Kolonaki does not have the orchestra background of the buses, but neither has it the fumes. Syntagma pavement cafes are mostly in the centre of the square, and although service is slower at these, there really is no reason for hurry on a fine evening. It is mostly European coffee (Nescafé) which is sold there. The traditional Turkish style, served with a glass of water, is sold in many places, and prices vary with the smartness (or otherwise) of the location. There are four ways of drinking Greek/Turkish coffee. *Sketos* is without sugar, *metrios* is medium sweet, *varisglikis* is strong and sweet, *glikis vrastos* is sweet and boiled. You will need the glass of water.

If you have plenty of time to spare, go to the open-air cafe in the Zappeion Gardens. On a fine evening, it is pleasant there, because of its practically unobstructed view of the Acropolis, the skyline of which one never tires. But if you find that cafe life is palling, and you want to attack the brighter lights, it is the Plaka again, or a journey out to Glyfada, or to Microlimano. Nightclubs in the western style are abundant, but it is the plaintive Bouzoukia which attracts the visitor. Fashions change so much in nightclubs of all types. Follow your ears, or the advice of the ever useful hotel hall porter (who incidentally is not averse to the occasional tip!). Bouzoukia is like retsina, an acquired taste, but in addition there are sweet singers from all over Greece, mandolin or guitar players, and the melodies are catching . . . feet tap, and before you know it, you are throwing caution to the winds and learning the intricate steps of the *syrtaki* from the nods, tugs and pushes of enthusiastic locals.

Once upon a time, the customers showed their approval of the musicians by smashing plates on the floor, and a patient little man constantly plied broom and pan to remove the debris. Don't re-start the practice. It is 'officially' frowned upon these days, and in any case, remember you are inevitably paying for the replacement of all the china! I find the Plaka atmosphere too spurious these days, and much prefer the more authentic atmosphere at Piraeus, or at the country tavernas, where one is more likely to find the spontaneity necessary to start an unforgettable evening. You will have to be patient. People dine very late in Greece and sit even later. It may well be around 12.30 before any sign of dancing begins, and it may not, even then. It is, after all, the unexpected which is the best.

Appendix I

Main bus routes

1 Attikis Square, Larissa St Omonia Square — Kallithea (trolley)
2 Kipseli, — Amalias — Nat. Museum — Patission (trolley)
3/7 Patission — Nat. Museum — Sofias — Ampelokipoi (trolley or bus)
5 Larissa — Omonia — Amalias — Kallithea (trolley)
10 Votanikos — Assomaton — Monastiraki — Syntagma — Ippokratus (bus)
12 Koliatsou — Omonia — Syntagma — Nat. Museum — Patission — Pangrati (trolley)
50 Kaningos — Akademia — Kolonaki — Likavitos (Lycabettus) (bus)

Useful suburban bus routes

1 Othonos — Edem — Kalamaki — Airport (West Air Terminal. Direct bus to East Air Terminal from 4 Amalia Ave.
25 Kaningos — Kifissia
30 Academy — Syngrou — Glifada (or Glyphada or Glifhada)
39 University — Sofias — Kaisariani
44 Assomaton — Dionysus Areop — Olgas O Konstandinou — Liopesi
45 Same continuing to Spata
46 Same continuing to Koropi
47 National Library — Physiko
62 Veranzerou — Plato's Academy
68 Eleftherias — Eleusis
70 Omonia — Piraeus
84 Olgas — Voula also to Glyfada
89 Olgas — Vouliagmeni
90 Olgas — Varkiza
100 Eleftherias — Dafni — Skarmangas

Long distance buses to Sounion, Lavrion, Marathon, and Porto Rafti depart from Mavromateion This street runs parellel to Patission from the Nat. Arch. Museum.

Long distance buses to the Peloponnese, Western Greece, Thrace etc. depart from Kifissou reached on 62 bus from Omonia.

Long distance buses to the Peloponnese, Western Greece, Southern Macedonia, depart from Liossion (reached on buses 63 and 34 from Syntagma and Omonia and buses 113, and 114, from Victor Hugo)

APPENDIX II

Some Useful Greek Terms

Acropolis — highest point of city with principal buildings
Agora — market or meeting place
Asklepeion — sanctuary of the god Asklepeios the Healer
Caique — fishing boat
Hephaisteion — temple of the god Hephaistos
Heraion — temple or sanctuary of the goddess Hera
Heroon — shrine of a hero or demi-god
Hieron — sanctuary
Kaffeneion — café/bar
Kastro — castle or fortress
Khora — place, usually principal place
Kouros — boy or statue of a youth
Medresseh — Moslem theological college
Meltemi — north wind
Moni — monastery or nunnery
Odeum — recital hall (Romanisation of odeion)
Pantokrator — the Christian God
Plateia — village or town square
Propylaia — sanctuary entrance or gateway
Souvlakia — grilled skewered meat
Stoa — free-standing portico or colonnaded walkway
Taverna — simple eating house
Tholoi — circular tombs

Archaeological periods

Neolithic	before 3000 B.C.
Pre-Hellenic or Bronze Age	3000-1100 B.C. (includes Minoan on Crete, Helladic on mainland, and Cycladic on islands)
Mycenaén	1400-1100 B.C. (contemporary with late pre-Hellenic)
Archaic	800-500 B.C.
Hellenistic	300-146 B.C.
Greco-Roman	146 B.C.-330 A.D.
Byzantine	330-1204 A.D.